ISBN 978-1-330-36710-0
PIBN 10041113

English
Français
Deutsche
Italiano
Español
Português

www.forgottenbooks.com

Mythology Photography **Fiction**
Fishing Christianity **Art** Cooking
Essays Buddhism Freemasonry
Medicine **Biology** Music **Ancient
Egypt** Evolution Carpentry Physics
Dance Geology **Mathematics** Fitness
Shakespeare **Folklore** Yoga Marketing
Confidence Immortality Biographies
Poetry **Psychology** Witchcraft
Electronics Chemistry History **Law**
Accounting **Philosophy** Anthropology
Alchemy Drama Quantum Mechanics
Atheism Sexual Health **Ancient History**
Entrepreneurship Languages Sport
Paleontology Needlework Islam
Metaphysics Investment Archaeology
Parenting Statistics Criminology
Motivational

FROM GRIEG TO BRAHMS

STUDIES OF SOME MODERN COMPOSERS AND THEIR ART

—

BY

DANIEL GREGORY MASON

NEW YORK
THE OUTLOOK COMPANY
1902

To my uncle
Dr. William Mason
who has won the gratitude
of lovers of music in America
I dedicate these studies
with affection and respect

PREFACE

—

⚜

"MUSIC may be hard to understand, but musicians are men;" so remarked a friend of mine when I was first planning these essays. The sentence sums up very happily a truth I have constantly had in mind in writing them. As all music, no matter what its complexity on the technical side, is in essence an expression of personal feeling, and as the qualities of a man's personality show themselves not only in his works, but in his acts, his words, his face, his handwriting and carriage even, it has seemed natural and fruitful, in these studies, to seek acquaintance with the musicians through acquaintance with the men.

But personal expression depends not alone

on the personality of the artist; it depends also on the resources of art, which in turn are the product of a long, slow growth. Accordingly, if we would understand the individual composers, we must have a sense of the scheme into which they fall, the great universal evolution of which they are but incidents. It is for this reason that I have tried, in the introductory essay on The Appreciation of Music, to describe some of the fundamental principles of the art, and to sketch in their light the general movement of musical history, in order to give the reader a perspective sense, a bird's-eye view of the great army of artists in which the supreme masters are but leaders of battalions and regiments. Without this sense it is impossible truly to place or justly to estimate any individual.

At the end of the introduction I apply the principles worked out to determining in a general way how the half dozen composers to be studied are related to modern music as a whole. My result is that although they are practically contemporary, they are by no means peers in the scope and significance of their work. If we arrange them in the order of their influence on art, which depends upon their power both to assimilate previous resources and to add new ones, we must pass " from Grieg to Brahms."

The purpose of the last essay in the book, on The Meaning of Music, will be obvious enough. Just as the introductory essay tries to sketch the general musical environment, as determined by basic principles and developed in history, in relation to which alone the individuals discussed can be understood, so the epilogue seeks to suggest that still larger environment of human feeling and activity on which music, like everything else, depends for its vitality. The first essay considers music as a medium for men, the last considers life as a medium for music.

It would be impossible to acknowledge here all that these studies, particularly the first, owe to the writings of others. Perhaps the books which have most influenced my treatment of musical æsthetics are Dr. George Santayana's " Sense of Beauty" and Dr. C. Hubert H. Parry's " Evolution of the Art of Music," though I have got much help also from Dr. William James's "Principles of Psychology," from Dr. Josiah Royce's books, from Mr. Edward Carpenter, and of course from Helmholtz, Gurney, Mr. W. H.

Hadow, and the other standard writers on musical theory. In gathering the biographical material I have had much cordial and skillful help from Miss Barton, of the Boston Public Library, for which I here record my thanks.

Cambridge, Massachusetts,
August 23, 1902.

CONTENTS

—

LIST OF ILLUSTRATIONS

—

INTRODUCTION
THE APPRECIATION
OF MUSIC

I
INTRODUCTION
THE APPRECIATION
OF MUSIC

HOWEVER interesting may be the study of an art through the personalities of the artists who have produced it, and such study, since art is a mode of human expression, is indeed essential, it must be supplemented by at least some general knowledge of the long continuous evolution in which the work of the most brilliant individual is but a moment, a phase. The quality of a man's work in art, and especially, as will be seen in a moment, in music, depends not alone on the depth of his character and the force of his talent, but also largely on the technical resources he owes to others, on the means for expressing himself that he finds ready to his hand. Whatever his personal powers or limitations, the value of his work will be determined not more by these than by the helps and hindrances of his artistic inheritance.

The great edifice of art, in fact, is like those Gothic cathedrals on which generations of men successively labored; thousands of common workmen hewed their foundation stones; finer minds, architects, smiths, brass founders, glass makers and sculptors wrought and decorated the superstructures; and the work of each, whatever his personal skill and devotion, was valuable only because it built upon and added to that of all the rest. The soaring spires are firmly based on blocks of stone ploddingly adjusted; the windows, often of such a perfect beauty that they seem created rather than constructed, had nevertheless to be built up bit by bit; and all the marvelous organism of pillars, arches and buttresses is so delicately solid, so precariously stable, that had one stress been miscalculated, one joint inaccurately made, the whole would collapse. So it is with the edifice of art, and particularly with that of music, which depends for its very material on the labors of musicians. Pigments, clay, marble, the materials of the plastic arts, exist already in the world; but the whole ladder of fixed tones on which music is built is the product of man's æsthetic sense, and had to be created slowly and laboriously by many generations of men. The successions of chords which every banjo player strums in his accompaniments were the subject of long trial by the mediæval composers. The hymn tune that any boy can write is modeled on a symmetrical scheme of phrases developed by countless experimenters. It took men centuries to select and arrange the eight tones of the ordinary scale, and centuries more to learn how to combine them in chords. And the most eloquent modern works depend on this long evolution of resources just as inevitably as the Gothic spire rests on the hewn stones so carefully laid. In the art, as in the cathedral, the seen rests upon the unseen, the beautiful upon the solid, the complex upon the simple, the new upon the old. The product of a thousand artists, music is as dependent on each as the coral reef on the tiny indispensable body of each insect; and on the other hand the individual musician, whatever his ability, is great only as he uses the equipment his fellows have prepared — "the greatest is the most indebted man."

If, then, we would justly value the half dozen

composers who have done most for music in our day, we must add to our understanding of them as persons a knowledge of the general development in which they play a part ; we must gain some sense of that great process of musical growth from which they inherit their resources, to which they make their various contributions, and in relation to which alone they can be fairly compared and appreciated. After examining the general course of musical history, ascertaining some fundamental principles, and applying these principles to our special judgments, we shall be able to perceive the greatest musicians of our day in their relations, and to get a perspective view of modern music in which they shall take their proper places.

I

IF we wish to get an idea of primeval music, to see from what impulses it took rise, we have only to study the musical activities of children and savages, in whom we have primeval man made contemporary, the remote past brought conveniently into the present to be observed. When we make such a study we find that both children and savages express their feelings by gestures and cries, that under the sway of emotion they either dance or sing. To them quiet, silent feeling is impossible. Are they joyful, they leap and laugh; are they angry, they strike and shout; are they sad, they rock and moan. Moreover, we can discriminate the kinds of feeling that are expressed by these cries and gestures. Roughly speaking, bodily movement is the natural outlet of active vitality, of the joy of life and the lust of living, while it is the more contemplative emotions—love, grief, reverie, devotion—that find vocal utterance. The war-dances and revels of savages, accompanied by drum and tomtom, are gesticulatory; their love-songs and ululations over the dead are vocal. In the same way children in their moments of enthusiasm are wont to march about shouting and stamping in time, all their limbs galvanized with nervous force; and it is when the wave of energy has passed and they sit on the floor engrossed in blocks or dolls that they sing to themselves their curious undulating chants. Even in ourselves we can observe the same tendencies, checked though they be by counter-impulses in our more complex temperaments: when we are gay we walk briskly, clicking our heels in time and perhaps whistling a catch; in our dreamier hours we are quiet, or merely hum a tune under our breath.   Thus through all human nature runs the tendency to vent feeling, active and contemplative, in those bodily movements and vocal utterances which underlie the two great generators of music, dance and song.

Such activities, however, are by no means as yet dance and song.   At first they are no more than mere reflex actions, as spontaneous and unthinking as the " Ow " of the man who stubs his toe.   The emotion is felt, and out comes the gesture or cry; that is all.   It is the organism's way of letting off steam.   It is not expression, not being prompted by a desire to communicate the feeling, but merely by the impulse to be unburdened of it.   Before there can be true expression or communication, there must be two more links added to the chain of which these automatic activities are only the first. The second link is imitation.   According to a theory widely exploited in recent years, we tend to imitate whatever we see another do.   With children the tendency is so strong that a large part of their time and energy is devoted to elaborate impersonation and make-believe, and the entire basis of their education is acquired through this directly assimilative faculty. In adults it is less active, but every sensitive person knows how difficult it is not to imitate foreign accents, stammering, and other petty mannerisms, and few are so callous that they can withstand the infection of strong stimuli like the gestures and cries of emotion. The wailing baby in the street car, who moves all the other babies within hearing to wail also (if they be not already at it independently) ; the dog baying the moon until all within earshot join in the serenade ; the negro at the camp-meeting clapping his hands until the whole company is in a rhythmic ecstasy—these are examples of the contagion of cries and gestures. Bearing them in mind, it is easy to see that the vocal or bodily acts which in the first place are mere reflexes of feeling, performed with no thought of expression, but only for personal easement, will generally, nevertheless, prompt similar acts in others. The performances of the individual will not end with himself; thanks to the instinct of imitation, they will be very widely copied.

But now—and this is the third link of the chain—bodily acts set up mental states, and a man cannot gesticulate or vocalize without feeling the emotions of which his actions are, as we say, expressive. "We feel sorry because we cry," writes Professor William James in his brilliant, paradoxical way, "angry because we strike, afraid because we tremble;" and whether or not we agree with his extreme view that the mental state is entirely a reverberation of bodily disturbances, we cannot but realize that in all these cases executing the expression tends to give us the feeling. He who persistently smiles will end by being cheerful, and a moderate amount of sighing or groaning will make any one melancholy. Above all, the imitation of vocal movements, such as we all go through at least incipiently when we hear melody, and the "keeping time" that strong dance-music so irresistibly prompts—these actions very noticeably set up in us their appropriate states of feeling. We not only imitate the lip motions and throat contractions of a persuasive speaker or singer, but doing so fills us with the emotion that prompts his utterance. Tired soldiers not only step out to a potently rhythmical tune—that is, they not only imitate the beat—but they actually feel less weary, more energetic, so long as the stimulus lasts. Once a bodily activity is set up, no matter how, it arouses the mental state proper to it ; in a word, expression generates emotion.

Obviously, then, if in the first place the natural outlets of emotional excitement are bodily motions and vocal sounds, if in the second place the observation of such motions and sounds arouses the impulse to imitate them, and if finally this imitation produces again in the imitator the states of mind which first set the whole process going, then these motions and sounds, these inchoate germs of dance and song, possess an enormous latent power of expression, and need only to be systematized to become a wonderfully eloquent language. Such a language, in fact, is music.

II

At this point, however, it is important not to go too fast. These crude gestures and cries by which primeval man expressed his feelings, though they were the germs out of which music grew, were as yet no more music, which is not only expressive sound, but formed, articulate sound, than an infant's cooings are speech. So far they were mere ebullitions, purposeless and formless; before they could become communicative they must become definite, they must take on some organic structure. Now gestures, bodily movements, are very easily grouped together by means of accent. Every walker knows that it is difficult not to emphasize alternate steps, grouping the unaccented with the accented into a cluster of two. Every waltzer makes a similar grouping of three steps, one accented, the other two subordinate. Some such system of grouping is instinctively adopted whenever we have a series of impressions regularly recurring in time. Let the reader, listening to the ticking of a watch, note how impossible it is to attend to each tick by itself. He will inevitably group them in twos; the accent may come on the first or on the last of the group, but he cannot hear them as exactly equal, any more than in walking he can put exactly equal stress on each step. It was this tendency of the mind to group its impressions on a basis of equal time measurements and unequal accents that led at the dawn of musical history to meter or rhythm, which is as persistent in music as it is in poetry. Metrical form was the natural means of giving definition to bodily movements, and as soon as it was developed enough to produce regular, easily imitated steps out of the chaotic gestures of naïve feeling, Dance was born.

At first, of course, metrical form was stumbled upon blindly. Having two arms and two legs, men naturally moved with a symmetry that gradually impressed their minds; obliged by the facts of anatomy to group their motions in twos, they soon took the hint, and beat their drums or struck their cymbals accordingly. The primeval dance was doubtless the march. But soon they began to carry out the principle they had thus chanced upon, and despite anatomy devised the group of three. The existence of triple meter is all the proof needed that metrical form is essentially a process of intelligence, not a physical fatality ; men grouped their steps or leaps or drum-taps in twos or in threes because such groups were easy to make, to imitate, and to remember. And once perceived, no matter how, such groupings tended to cling, to perpetuate themselves. For they were definite, memorable forms, and they survived all haphazard gestures and vague motions by virtue of the law that what is adapted to its environment will live longer than what is not. In this case the environment was the human mind ; and the definite organisms, the metrical forms, survived and developed because the mind could remember them, while all the vague gestures out of which they grew shared the fate of what is indefinite, accidental, inorganic. Thus Dance, which was gesticulation systematized by metrical form, emerged and grew in the human mind, like an animal in a congenial habitat.

For a long while the metrical forms that men could perceive and remember were most rudimentary. Probably it took them centuries to grasp the simple group of three, the basis of such accent-schemes as the waltz and the mazurka. Even to-day, psychologists agree, we are unable to grasp a group of seven, and we perceive larger groups than three only as compounded of the elementary twos and threes.* But gradually men learned to recombine their groups in still larger forms, of which the first

* Thus " 4/4 time " is a compound of twos, " 6/8 time " is a compound of threes, and the interesting 5/4 measure, so effective in the second movement of Tschaikowsky's Pathetic Symphony, is a compound of twos and threes regularly alternating.

groups constituted the elements.   Just as in
chemistry the basic elements like oxygen and
hydrogen, nitrogen and carbon, can combine
only in a few simple ways, but the compound
molecules thus produced can recombine into
the myriad substances of organic chemistry, the
sugars and starches and all the rest, so the simple dual and triple measures of music can be
built into an infinite variety of figures and
phrases.   In early dance and folk-song a more
and more complex metrical plan thus slowly
developed.   Two or more of the simple groups
of beats, called measures, were combined into
a larger group, a recognizable figure or motif;
then again motifs were combined into still
larger phrases ; and finally, as the musical medium became more definite, plastic and various,
phrases were combined in many different types
of design, into complete " tunes."   In all these
regroupings, the wonderful variety of which is
one of the most precious resources of modern
music, the fundamental procedure was the same
—elements alike in duration, but different in
accent or significance, were made to cohere in
a group or form.   Just as in verse the feet, or
elementary metrical forms whose elements are

single syllables of equal duration but unequal stress, are combined into lines, and later these lines into stanzas, so in music measures are combined in figures, and figures built up into phrases, and phrases into tunes. And as the diversity of the possible forms becomes greater and greater as we advance from foot to stanza, there being few forms of feet but many of stanza, so metrical form in music becomes more and more complex as it evolves, and though all music must be built out of dual or triple measures, it may be built into tunes of an infinite variety of pattern. Each new complexity, however, must be intelligible ; it cannot be introduced until men have mastered the simpler groups out of which it is compounded. Beethoven's wondrously intricate texture, Brahms's soaring phrases, would be meaningless to us had we not inherited from thousands of ancestors a sense of the system of regular accents and duration on which their complexities are superposed. From the days, ages ago, when savages first beat a drum in simple march rhythm, up to to-day, when Brahms builds up his extraordinarily intricate fabrics, with their elaborate prosody, their " augmentation," and "diminution," and "shifted rhythm," the evolution of metrical form has been single and continuous; each advance has been built on previous achievements. There are no dropped stitches in this kind of knitting.

Metrical form, however, is not the only sort of form by which sounds can be combined. It is the natural organizing agent of Dance, which, as we have seen, develops out of the movements expressive of men's active impulses; but human nature has also its contemplative side, and this, expressing itself in vocal utterance, undergoes another sort of development and results in Song. What, then, are the means by which Song is defined, by which vocal sounds are organized into intelligible and memorable forms? Before we answer this question it will be well to consider for a moment a more general one. What, in general, is a form?

We shall be helped to define a form in general by looking back to the metrical forms we have just been studying. These, we have seen, are groups or clusters of impressions, held together by some similarity, yet also differentiated by some contrast. The two or three beats of the measure-group are similar in duration, yet different in accent. And without both the similarity and the difference, the unity and the variety, they would not be a group. Without similarity they would be a haphazard collection, a chaos; without difference they would all fuse together in one indistinguishable mass. In other words, they exemplify a general fact about forms—namely, that the elements must be alike enough to be associated, and yet different enough to be discriminated. If we cannot associate them we cannot feel them as a group; they will not cohere. If, on the other hand, we cannot discriminate them, then do they equally fail to make up a form; they simply mingle together into a homogeneous lump. The organs of an organism must be, then, related, yet different; the elements of a form must be both similar and dissimilar. Unless they are both we cannot perceive them as linked, yet distinct. Bearing this general fact about forms in mind, we may investigate the kinds of form that underlie Song.

Probably every one who has listened to the whistling of factories in a large city at noon has had the curious experience of suddenly hearing amid the meaningless din a pair of tones that mysteriously mate and merge. The other tones seem entirely accidental; they have no relation to each other, and give one merely a sense of vague annoyance. But these two form an intelligible group; we are able to grasp them together, and we take an indescribable pleasure in thus feeling them as parts of one whole. Here is an instance of another sort of musical form than the metrical, a sort that we may call harmonic. Here the grouping takes place on a platform not of time, but of pitch; the two elements of the group have no metrical relations, but in pitch they are somehow related. Now this sort of pitch relationship has played a vital part in music, a part hardly secondary to that of time relationship; so that an understanding of it is important enough to delay us here a moment with some rather dry technical facts on which it depends.

Ordinary musical tones, the notes of the voice, the violin, and the piano, for example, simple as they sound, are, like ordinary white light, rather complex compounds of many simple elements. There are in them seven or eight constitutent or " partial " tones, quite distinctly audible to the trained ear or to the untrained ear armed with suitable instruments; and these partial tones, produced by vibrations in the sound-emitting body whose rates are regularly related, bear a certain fixed relation to each other, like the spectrum-colors that compose white light. Not only this, but each partial tone arouses its own proper sensation in the ear by stimulating there one of the minute filaments called the cords of Corti, each of which vibrates sympathetically to a tone of given pitch and to no other. Now we are to imagine that when an ordinary musical tone is sounded, seven or eight of these little cords immediately start a-tremble, and send to the brain their messages, which combine there into the composite impression we name "a tone." If now another tone is sounded, one which starts into motion another set of filaments, and if furthermore there is one filament now set in motion that was also excited by the first compound tone—if, in other words, the two tones happen to have a partial tone in common, which in both instances excites the same filament in the ear, then we shall have a sense of close relationship between them; they will make together a harmonic group or form. This, as a matter of fact, is what happens with any two tones that form what is called a consonant interval with each other, an "octave," a "fifth," or a "fourth." If tones X and Y, for instance, are an octave apart, the second partial tone of X will be identical with the first of Y; if they are a fifth apart, the third partial tone of X will be identical with the second of Y; if they are a fourth apart, the fourth partial tone of X will correspond with the third of Y. It is obvious, then, that all these intervals will give us the sense of harmonic form; for they provide all the necessary conditions of a form, having enough in common to be associated by our minds, and enough not in common (their dissimilar partial tones) to be distinguished. When the partial tone in common is so high, and therefore so weak, that it impresses us but slightly, we shall have little or no sense of their being related; such is the case in the so-called imperfect consonances and the dissonances. When, on the other hand, all the most prominent partial tones of one exist in the other, they will fuse into one impression in our minds, losing the characteristic of form entirely, as is the case to some extent with the octave and entirely with the unison. But when, as in the case of fifths and fourths, there are both a distinctly audible partial tone in common and others not in common, then we shall have true harmonic forms.

So much technical detail will be forgiven by the reader who can at all realize how profoundly the entire history of music has been affected by these acoustic and physiological facts. We have already seen how folk - music slowly wrought out the complex metrical forms based upon time grouping. In the same way, ecclesiastical music wrought out, slowly and laboriously, the harmonic and melodic forms that were based upon pitch-grouping. For a long time vocal utterance was defined only by certain simple intervals like the fall of the fourth, which formed the cadences of Greek dramatic recitation and of mediæval Christian intoning. Gradually ornamental notes were introduced as approaches to the final note; these were varied in pitch, and new ones added, until finally there resulted the ancient modes, precursors of our scale. Then, when two melodies began to be sung at once, the intervals of the octave, fifth, and fourth were again called into requisition, and made the bases of primitive harmony. In the old Organum of the Middle Ages, two voices, a fifth apart, gave the same melody, just as with the Greeks, in the process called "magadising," two voices sang the same tune, an octave apart. So, step by step, pitch relations were perceived and utilized. In all stages of the long progress, whether the interval chosen was the octave or the fifth or the fourth, and whether the tones were sounded in succession as a melodic step or simultaneously as a chord, the guiding principle was the same; tones were grouped together which had pitch-form, which had partial tones in common and others not in common. A harmonic form, like a metrical form, was always a cluster of tones that could be both associated and distinguished.

It was a long time before these two means of organizing sound were used in combination. Until the seventeenth century metrical form was chiefly used, quite naturally, to define the gesticulatory part of musical material, the product of active emotion, while harmonic form gave coherence to the vocal part, the product of contemplative or religious emotion. Primitive dance either neglected pitch relationship entirely, as in that kind of savage music which uses

only drums, tomtoms, clappers and such per-
cussive instruments, or used only the simplest
intervals like the fall of the fourth or the rise of
the fifth. And in ecclesiastical Song, all through
the Middle Ages, metrical regularity was not
only not sought for—it was avoided. Even in
the highly artistic song of the great choral epoch
which culminated in Palestrina there was no
rhythm. Phraseology depended entirely on
the words. Composers avoided anything like
an appearance of even sections, in sharp de-
marcation, balancing each other, such as we now
demand. They liked rather to have their melodies cross and interlace like the strands in a
basket, making a texture solid but inorganic.
To them coherence was a matter merely of
the individual voices ; music held together
like a rope rather than like a crystal. Indeed, any deeper harmonic unity was not
feasible until they had gained more experience in tone relationship. But eventually the
secular composers of the last half of the
seventeenth century, among whom Arcangelo
Corelli is a typical figure, learned to utilize both
kinds of form, making them supplement and
reënforce each other in all sorts of interesting

and unexpected ways. With Corelli, pure music emerges as an independent art, beautiful as sculpture and promising new powers of expression By his successors this new promise was realized with surprising rapidity. Constantly growing more independent of extraneous aids, developing, thanks to the fruitful interaction of metrical and harmonic grouping, an unprecedented richness and variety, music became in the hands of Bach and Beethoven a strong, flexible and efficient fabric, adapted to all phases of expression and capable of forming the most complex and self-sufficient structures. Evolved from the crude gestures and cries of naïve feeling by a never-ceasing, ever-widening exertion of man's intelligence, absolute music has become in some respects the most eloquent and penetrative of the arts.

III

FORM in music, however, notwithstanding its origin as a means of defining those emotional expressions which without it would have remained vague, unimitable, and immemorable, is much more than a means of definition. At first practiced as a means to an end, it soon became an end in itself. For the perception of relations, the mental activity which groups impressions, is not merely useful ; it is profoundly, indescribably delightful. Calling the mind into activity just as sensation calls the senses, it is a far deeper source of pleasure than sensation can ever be, because the mind far exceeds the senses in the subtlety, variety and independence of its action. When, therefore, the primitive musicians first made their syntheses of gestures and cries they discovered a novel pleasure, altogether more delicious than the crude joys of sensation and expression. Before they made such syntheses they had merely enjoyed the sweetness of tones, and taken satisfaction in expressing their feelings; but when once they learned to group their expressive tones together, to feel the subtle bonds which bound them into clear and salient unity, then they felt a joy altogether new and on a higher plane, they felt true æsthetic delight. Here was not merely a passive, or at most an automatic process ; here was a truly creative activity, a conscious and free manipulation of materials. Mere hearing, however delicious, mere expression, however grateful, could not give this sense of mastery, of comprehension, of insight. Beauty alone, beauty depending on consciously made comparisons and contrasts, can give the highest æsthetic delight, the delight in form. And so, like painters who, using form at first to define their material, come quickly to a realization of its inherent value, and finally, if they be true artists, value its pure beauties of line and balance and composition more highly than any mere richness of color or of expression, musicians, in the degree of their true musicianship, came to prize the intrinsic beauty of music above all its other qualities.

Sometimes, doubtless, they carried their devotion too far. In certain periods and individuals the love of formal beauty has entirely eclipsed pleasure in expression. Unable to attend at once to expression and to beauty, many composers, and in some periods all, have devoted their entire energy to the quest for formal perfection. Thus in the work of the Netherland masters of early counterpoint, in some of Bach's ingenious weavings, and in much of the music of Haydn and his contemporaries, the search for purely plastic qualities goes on with little thought of the original emotional burden of the material that is being formulated. To such men form was much more than a means of defining expression ; it was an end in itself, and an end worth a lifetime of painstaking, devoted effort.

And yet, justifiable as their feeling was, indispensable as their labors were to that development without which the expressive power of music would itself have remained rudimentary, it is not to their view, but to a more universal one, that we must look to find a rounded theory of expression and form. If it be a mistake to neglect the latter for the former, as they well saw, it is equally a mistake to prize form with too exclusive an enthusiasm. For beauty is itself one of the most potent means of expression. Our minds are not made up of hermetic compartments, but are so permeable, so conductive, that an eloquent thing is made more eloquent by being also beautiful. The impression of beauty reverberates endlessly, intensifying all that is associated with it. The general atmosphere transfigures every feature. If the whole is fair, no detail will be entirely without its appeal to our kindled imaginations, but if the whole is formless, no single phrase, however impassioned, can affect us very deeply. The truth is, then, that form and expression in music are as essential to each other as objects and light in the world of vision. No radiance of illumination will satisfy the eye if there is nothing to see, and, on the other hand, the loveliest things will give little pleasure in the dark. To be beautiful they must be suffused in light. Similarly the phrases of music, to be truly moving, must be suffused in beauty. The greatest masters clearly realized this. Bach in his masterpieces, Beethoven nearly always, and Brahms in his inspired hours, acted on the principle that the two elements must exist side by side, subtly and potently reacting upon each other. Their practice, indeed, unanimously confirms the theory of musical effect which has now been briefly sketched, and which may be more briefly summarized before we pass on to deduce from it some general canons of appreciation and criticism.

Music, we have seen, originates in the spontaneous gestures and cries made by primitive man under the sway of emotion, imitated by observers, and arousing in them the same feelings. As intelligence dawns, men see that this triple process of spontaneous action, imitation and reduplicated feeling affords a basis for a language of emotion, a language that needs, however, to be somehow defined and articulated. Articulation gradually follows by means of the grouping in time which develops the gestures of active feeling into Dance, and the grouping in pitch which develops the utterances of contemplative feeling into Song. Eventually the two modes of grouping are combined, and music becomes an independent art. Meanwhile, the forms at first adopted for the sake of mere definitiòn become the basis of a new and deeper delight, æsthetic beauty, which is sought for both as ancillary to expression and for itself alone. Finally, beauty of form reacts potently on eloquence of expression, and the most universal composers, recognizing the interdependence of the two elements, produce the highest type of pure music, music in which beauty is based upon expression and expression transfigured by beauty.

IV

THE principles we now have before us, interesting as they are in themselves, must finally vindicate their worth by helping us to form sound opinions of musical tendencies and of individual composers; they must provide a corrective for the whims and freaks of prejudice, and a basis for that intelligent and systematic criticism which takes account both of a man's qualities and of his defects before assigning him his place in the general artistic movement. With them in mind, we should be able to avoid the current one-sided and partial views, and also to attain that positive insight into the nature of music which alone can give our opinions sanity, liberality and perspective.

In the first place, then, it will be well to turn their light on certain dangerous half-truths, which, constantly cropping up in musical opinions, are hardly less misleading than complete fallacies. The two most persistent and mischievous of such half-truths are those which neglect one aspect of the dual nature of music, which ignore expression or repudiate form. Of the first, the half-truth so frequently formulated in the phrase, " Music is a kind of audible mathematics," it is not necessary to say much. Those dryly ingenious persons who rejoice in a fugue of Bach much as they enjoy an intricate problem in calculus, failing to perceive the warm human heart that animates the skeleton, form a minority which gets little attention from the mass of music-lovers. The half-truth which neglects expression will not, in the nature of things, ever gain a large following. Far more dangerous is the opposite fallacy, which, repudiating form, asserts that expression is all, that "music is the language of the emotions." This phrase, without any qualifications, is the creed of the sentimentalists. Their ranks assemble all varieties of rhapsodical, ill-balanced temperaments, from the young girl who "dotes on Wagner" to the old lady with curls who thinks that "music leads us up to the higher life." The sentimentalists sin, perhaps, not so much by commission as by omission. So far as they are able they appreciate music, for they feel it emotionally, and, as we have seen, half its reason for being is its appeal to the emotions. But they fail to realize that it must be beautiful as well as moving, that all its lineaments of expression must be held in orderly relation with a larger integral beauty of form. They fancy that form, which in reality enhances expression, is somehow at odds with it, that the mind and the feelings are natural enemies. Satisfied with thrills and tremors, they do not ask, in their music, for meaning and order. They fancy that to listen heedfully, attentively, analytically, is somehow to pull out the petals of art and strew them in the dust. Analysis is a desecrating process. You should not focus your ears, make the image clear; you should swoon in a delicious haze of sensation and suggestion. But one can analyze without dissecting; one can recognize that a flower has petals without pulling them out; and indeed it is hard to imagine any one appreciating the true loveliness of a flower, its formed, articulated beauty, without such recognition. So in music, the true lover of melody will be in no danger of confusing Beethoven's Hymn of Joy with Schumann's *Warum* because of the trance of nebulous feeling into which they throw him. He will pay them the tribute of listening to them attentively, of noting the various charms of their phraseology and expression as he would note the difference of meter and effect between a sonnet of Shakespeare and a song of Burns. Music is not poorer, but richer, for its marvelous intricacies of structure, and the sentimentality which hates clear definition is not high sentiment, but misconception or insensibility.

It is a suggestive fact, however, that the sentimental attitude is found among us, not only in music, but everywhere. It is the tendency of the day to confuse acquiring with assimilating, to fancy that wealth of experience is better than self-mastery and intelligent possession. Heedlessness is our besetting sin. We skim books, " do " picture galleries, talk at the opera, interrupt in conversation, and gobble our food. Metaphorically, as well as actually, we swallow more than we can digest, imagining that if we only subject ourselves to enough impressions we shall become connoisseurs. We value quantity rather than quality, in everything from bric-à-brac to education ; and it is quite to be expected that we should reckon the value of music by the number of shivers it can give us. But we are nevertheless capable of a wiser attitude. We have it in us to learn that feelings are of no use until they are related to the central personality, that impressibility is not yet dignity, that to be informed is not necessarily to be educated—that, in a word, possession of any sort is not an external fact, but an inward control. We may take a facile interest in the sentimentalists and the enthusiasts—the people with " temperament "—but at heart we know that those passions are deepest which are most firmly dominated by will, that he is freest who obeys the highest law, and that "temperament" is after all less vital than character. We really prefer organization to coruscation. And so in music we are capable of learning, and knowledge of the principles of musical effect can help us to learn, that the balance and proportion and symmetry of the whole is far more essential than any poignancy, however great, in the parts. He best appreciates music who brings to it all of his human powers, who understands it intellectually as well as feels it emotionally.

In these and other ways the principles of musical effect afford touchstones for the detection of prevalent but erroneous views—views which contain their element of truth, but are still fallacious because partial. But the same principles are also capable of yielding more positive and detailed insight into the nature of musical appreciation. They illuminate, for example, that perplexing problem of expression— why it is that from the same piece of music one person gets so much more than another. The

fact is familiar to every one. Every one knows
that of two persons equally sensitive to music
on the sensuous and formal side, of good " ear,"
and familiar with the effects of harmony, melody and rhythm, one will get far deeper mean-
ings, will be far more elated and inspired, than
the other. How can this be? Our theory of
expression gives the clew. We have seen that
bodily states set up by imitation are the basis
of musical emotions. Hearing is always a sort
of ideal performing. In listening to a melody
we always feebly contract our throat muscles as
if to sing, and the perception of rhythm is
always accompanied by an incipient " keeping
time." These bodily acts, however faintly
realized, set up their appropriate feelings, the
feelings we associate with their actual performance. But now it should be noted that the
richness, quality, and significance of these feelings will depend in the case of each man on his
particular associations—that is to say, on his
entire personal character. Evoked by similar
bodily states, the mental emotions will be always as dissimilar as the men who feel them.
" We cannot conceive," says Thoreau, " of a
greater difference than that between the life of

one man and that of another." He might
truly have added that we cannot conceive of a
greater difference than that between the feelings
of one man and those of another in hearing
the same piece of music, which excites in both
the same tremors and thrills, but vistas of
thought how utterly unlike! Musical appreciation is thus subject to the same variations
which make the ordinary experiences of men
so diverse. The prophet on fire with righteous
indignation and the common scold undergo in
anger the same suffusion of blood, the same
boiling up of the organs; yet how different in
dignity and value are their sentiments! And
music, by setting up a certain sympathetic tur-
moil in the organs, will plunge one man into a
selfish opium-dream and will fill another with
the rarest, most magnanimous aspirations. It
follows as a practical corollary that he who
would get from music the best it has to offer
must cultivate the best in himself. No fine
sensibility in him, no large heroism, no generosity or dignity or profundity of character
will be without its quiet, far-reaching effect on
his appreciation of music.

If expression depends thus in part upon the

moral and temperamental qualities of the listener, form in equal measure depends upon his mental alertness. "Form," says Dr. Santayana, "does not appeal to the inattentive; they get from objects only a vague sensation which may in them awaken extrinsic associations; they do not stop to survey the parts or to appreciate their relation, and consequently are insensible to the various charms of various unifications; they can find in objects only the value of material or of function, not that of form." This is unfortunately the case with many who consider themselves "musical"; they enjoy sweetness of sound and the rather vague emotion music arouses in them, but get no clear sense of its deeper architectural beauty. Like Charles Lamb, they are "sentimentally disposed to harmony, but organically incapable of a tune." But a thoroughgoing love of music, as will be clear enough by now, must include an appreciation of all its aspects; and since beauty of form is not only delightful in itself, but is a potent means of expression as well, insensibility to it involves the loss of much of what is most precious in music. It is necessary, then, to train the attention, to listen accurately as well as sympathetically, to grasp the thematic phrases as they occur, to remember them when they recur, and to follow them through all their transformations. We should think that man but slightly appreciative of poetry who, after hearing a play of Shakespeare, should say that the words seemed to him mellifluous and that many passages moved him, but that he had not the slightest idea what it was all about. Yet how many of us, after hearing a Beethoven symphony, have the slightest definite idea what it is about? If we would get more than transient, profitless titillation from music, we must cultivate our attention, learning, to borrow a phrase from optics, "to make the image sharp." As we progress in that faculty we shall constantly see new beauties, which in turn will constantly react to deepen expression; and if we are so fortunate as to have also a nature sensitive, tender, and earnest, fitted to feel the best kind of emotion that can be aroused by sound, we may hope to gain eventually an accurate, intelligent, and deep appreciation of music.

V

IT remains, now that we have traced the bearing of our general principles on musical taste, to point out briefly how they afford also criteria for judging composers themselves, and how, thus judged, the six composers we are to study fall into perspective. Our principles, in a word, will now enable us to supplement our later studies of these composers in isolation with a somewhat rough but still helpful sense of their interrelationship. We must relate them to the general evolution of which they are phases; see how they differ in the power to assimilate the work of their predecessors, to avail themselves of all the resources, expressive and formal, of their art, and to develop new resources for those who succeed them. It is hardly necessary to insist on the value of some such basis of comparison. Without it we should be like a certain member of a college geology class who, more ardent than methodical, was wont to investigate outcrops and moraines with great enthusiasm, but in utter ignorance of the points of the compass. To this scatter-brained young man the instructor used always to say, " Orient yourself first of all, Mr. Jones, orient yourself." And so, before examining the individual outcroppings of modern music, we shall do well to orient ourselves in the artistic landscape.

Of all the composers with whom we are to deal, Grieg and Dvořák are the least inclusive and catholic. Grieg, as we shall see, writes always in the personal vein, is among musicians what Leigh Hunt and Charles Lamb are among writers. He is intimate, charming, graceful, but never epic or universal. He touches the great stream of musical tradition at a few points only, and adds little to its volume. He knows how to combine a few elements of effect with finesse, but there are limitations both in what he has to say and in his means of saying it. He is familiar with only one dialect in the language of tones. And if Grieg is personal, Dvořák is at most national. He is too deep-dyed a Bohemian to be a complete citizen of the world. Not only is his style curiously provincial, with its uneven rhythms of folk-song, its strong dance-like metrical schemes, and its florid coloring, but his substance is too ornate and too sweet to be profoundly significant. He is a "natural" musician raised to the nth power, but he is not enough a scholar to relate himself very vitally with the general growth of his art. Both of these men have contributed much that is novel and charming to the lighter side of music, but they are not masters of deep feeling and wide scope.

Camille Saint-Saëns and César Franck illustrate strikingly another sort of partiality, a partiality often met with in a less noticeable degree. Each exemplifies only one of those contrasting phases of feeling which we saw to underlie Dance and Song, and which in the greatest composers are combined. Saint-Saëns' work, primarily expressive of active feeling, is strongly metrical, derives its chief interest and value from rhythmic qualities; Franck's, the product of a singularly contemplative and monastic nature, is monotonous in rhythm, but endlessly various in melodic and harmonic treatment. In the biographical essays the antithesis will be brought out more in detail. Here it is only necessary to suggest that, if these two French composers are somewhat wider in scope than Grieg or Dvořák, their curious limitations in temperament prevent them from doing all-inclusive and universal work.

With Tschaïkowsky and Brahms we come to men of a larger caliber. These two, different as they are—the Russian finding in music primarily a means of expression, the German

valuing more its plastic beauty—are, nevertheless, the only two moderns who can be said to
carry on worthily the torch of Bach and Beethoven. Both were men of sufficiently wide
sympathy and scholarship to approach music
with the utmost liberality, to get into contact
with all its traditions and utilize all its technical
resources. They write in that " grand style "
which draws its elements from the widest *universalist*
sources, the style not of one man nor of one
nation, but of the world. Again, they were
men of complex temperament, capable of a
great range of feeling both active and contemplative. Consequently the dance impulse and
the song impulse are equally operative in their
work, which has a richness and variety to be
found in Bach and Beethoven, but not in Saint-
Saëns or Franck. And though they were men
of the deepest emotion, they had also the intellectual control over their work that made it not
only expressive but beautiful. In a word, the
range of their learning, the manysidedness of
their temperaments, their emotional profundity
and their intellectual power, all conspired to
make them the greatest musicians of their
time.

Yet even between these two great men it is possible, with the aid of our principles, to make a distinction. We have seen that form is not only a means of defining utterance, but that it is furthermore the source of æsthetic delight, and, through the reverberation of that, of an immense reënforcement to expression; and we have accordingly concluded that in no case must form be sacrificed to any other factor of effect whatsoever. To sacrifice form, in music, whatever may seem at first sight the justification, is in the long run to sacrifice the greater for the less. Now Tschaïkowsky, led away by the impetuosity of his feeling, is often guilty of such a sacrifice. He gains for the moment; he gains a compelling eloquence, the most exciting effects, the wildest and most thrilling crises. But in the long run he loses. Eventually one tires of the crises, one is left cold, and then the waywardness, the incoherence, the lack of clear order and symmetry, are felt as weaknesses. Too many of Tschaïkowsky's pieces are better at a first hearing than at a fifth. With Brahms it is otherwise. All his emotion, deep, tender and noble as it is, is controlled by the firm will and the shaping hand of the supreme artist. However moving his music may be, it is even more beautiful. His faculties, whether by good fortune or merit, are more perfectly adjusted than those of any other modern composer. He is the most profound, the most simple, the most comprehensive of moderns, as becomes obvious when we test his work by the principles we have laid down. Others exemplify them partially, he most entirely; others are great in some or several effects, he is roundedly great. He allies himself with all that was done in music before him, and contributes indispensable elements to what will be done in it hereafter. And so, if we arrange our six composers in a series, determining the importance of each by means of the universal and impersonal principles of art, we must pass from Grieg to Brahms.

II
EDVARD GRIEG

EDVARD GRIEG

II
EDVARD GRIEG

TO the musical amateur no contemporary composer is better known than Grieg. Every school-girl plays his piano pieces, young violinists study his delightfully melodious sonatas, and few concert pieces are more widely loved than the Peer Gynt Suite. Yet from professional musicians Grieg does not meet with such favor. Many speak of him patronizingly, some scornfully. "Grieg?" they say. "Oh, yes, very charming, but—" and the sentence ends with a shrug. The reason for this discrepancy of estimate seems to be that the layman, fascinated by Grieg's lovely melodies, unusual and piquant harmonic treatment, and contagious rhythm, looks for no further quality; but the musician, unconsciously referring all music to a standard based on works of greater solidity, greater breadth and force and passion as well as wider learning and superior skill, is too conscious of the shortcomings of this Norwegian minstrelsy to do justice to its qualities. It is, of a truth, music in which merit and failing are curiously mingled; its delicate beauty is unique, its limitation extreme. It is as fair as a flower, and as fragile. It is, in short, the effluence of a personality graceful without strength, romantic without the sense of tragedy, highly gifted with all gentle qualities of nature, but lacking in the more virile powers, in broad vision, epic magnanimity, and massive force.

Of this personality, as it appears in the flesh, we get an interesting glimpse in Tschaïkowsky's Diary.* "During the rehearsal of Brahms's new trio," writes Tschaïkowsky, "as I was taking the liberty of making some remarks as to the skill and execution of the relative *tempo* 2–3— remarks which were very good-naturedly received by the composer—there entered the room a very short, middle-aged man, exceedingly

* "Diary of My Tour in 1888," translated in "Tschaïkowsky, His Life and Works," by Rosa Newmarch. (John Lane, New York, 1900.)

fragile in appearance, with shoulders of unequal height, fair hair brushed back from his forehead, and a very slight, almost boyish beard and mustache. There was nothing very striking about the features of this man, whose exterior at once attracted my sympathy, for it would be impossible to call them handsome or regular; but he had an uncommon charm, and blue eyes, not very large, but irresistibly fascinating, recalling the glance of a charming and candid child. I rejoiced in the depths of my heart when we were introduced to each other, and it turned out that this personality which was so inexplicably sympathetic to me belonged to a musician whose warmly emotional music had long ago won my heart. He proved to be the Norwegian composer, Edvard Grieg." This was in 1888, when Grieg was forty-five. We may compare with it another description, made a year later by a Frenchman, M. Ernest Closson, when Grieg was playing and conducting his works in Paris. " Grieg is small, thin, and narrow-shouldered," writes M. Closson.* " His body, which is like a child's, is always in motion—the

* " Edvard Grieg et la Musique Scandinave," Ernest Closson, Paris, Librairie Fischbacher, 1892.

movements short, lively, singularly jerky and angular, each step shaking the whole body and hitching the shoulder as if he limped; a 'bundle of nerves' ["*paquet des nerfs*"], to use a doctor's phrase of picturesque energy. The head, which looks massive on so small a body, is intelligent and very handsome, with long grayish hair thrown back, thin face, smooth-shaven chin, short, thick mustache, small but full nose, and eyes!—eyes superb, green, gray, in which one can fancy one catches a glimpse of Norway, with its melancholy fjords and its luminous mists. His gaze is serious, wonderfully soft, with a peculiar expression, at once worn, tentative, and childishly naïve. The entire effect is of kindness, gentleness, candor, a sincere modesty."

It is thus obvious that Grieg is of the nervous, sensitive temperament, the temperament of Keats and Stevenson, quick and ardent in feeling, and in art notable for subjective, intimate work rather than for the wide objective point of view. Grieg's music is of value, indeed, just because it is the artistic expression of delicate personal feeling. We shall find that his whole development tended toward a singularly individual, or at most national, utterance; that his efforts toward a complexer or more universal style, such as in poetry we call epic, were unsuccessful; and that his real and inimitable achievement is all in the domain of the pure lyric.

Edvard Grieg was born in Bergen, Norway, in 1843. At an early age he showed musical talent, starting in to learn the piano and theory at six, under his mother's direction. Gesine Grieg, born Hagerup, descendent from a forceful Norwegian family which had produced some famous men, was a woman of musical and poetic instinct and of strong character. She had studied music in Hamburg and in London, and given some concerts and many soirées in Bergen. In a word, her son could not have found a better guide in his first studies. At nine Grieg surprised his school-teacher by submitting in place of a literary composition a set of original variations on a German melody, a substitution which was not kindly received. He was told to stop such nonsense. The artistic temperament revealed itself also in great sensitiveness to the beauty of the somber Northern landscape, and at fifteen Grieg wished to become a painter. Fortunately, however, his musical ability was recognized by the famous violinist Ole Bull, at whose suggestion his parents decided to send him to the Leipsic Conservatory, whither he traveled in 1858. Here again the romanticism of the boy showed itself in his fretfulness under the strict régime of his masters, Hauptmann, Richter, Rietz, Reinecke, and Moscheles, and in his passionate devotion to the works of Schumann and Chopin, who were then looked upon in academic circles as somewhat dangerous revolutionaries. Except for a vacation of some months at home, necessitated by the pulmonary trouble which has ever since weakened Grieg's health, he spent four years in the Conservatory, being graduated in 1862.

In his earliest compositions, produced at this period, the traits that afterwards distinguished him are rather hampered by academic influences and uncertainty of intention. The four Pieces, opus 1, by no means devoid of his peculiar flavor, are yet tentative in style and reminiscent of older masters, particularly Chopin and Mendelssohn. Of the Poetic Tone-pictures, opus 3, the second and fourth are the well-established type of graceful *salon* piece. Number four, indeed, might almost be a strayed leaf from that gentle but hackneyed work which some modern cynic has called the " Songs without Music." Yet the very next piece is full-fledged Grieg. Here is the short four-measure phrase, transposed a third and repeated, here the descending chromatic harmonizations, here the raucous fifths as of peasant players, that we shall presently learn to look for among the hall-marks of his writings. But more important than any such technical details is the general animation, producing trenchant rhythm, graceful melody, and warm harmony, that always sparkles in Grieg's best work. In the Poetic Tone-pictures he is already himself, though not his mature self.

Being at graduation somewhat bewildered and uncertain as to his future course, Grieg turned his steps in 1863 to the Danish capital, the home of a great man whom he idolized. " One day," he writes in an autobiographical fragment, " I had gone out with my friend Matthison-Hansen to Klampenborg. Suddenly he nudged my arm.

" ' What is it ? ' I said.

" ' Do you see that little man with the large gray hat ? '

" ' I see him.'

" ' Do you know who it is ? ' said he.

" ' I haven't the least idea.'

" ' That's Gade,' he said. ' Shall I introduce you ? '

" And without waiting for my reply he took me up to the Professor, with the curt announcement :

" ' Professor, a Norwegian friend of mine— a good musician.'

" ' Is it Nordraak ? ' asked Gade.

" ' No, it is Grieg,' answered Matthison-Hansen.

" ' Oh, that's who it is,' said Gade, scanning my insignificant and humble self from head to foot with a searching glance, while I stood, not without awe, face to face with the man whose works I treasured so highly. ' Have you something to show me ? '

" ' No,' I answered. For the things I had finished didn't seem good enough.

" ' Then go home and write a symphony,' recommended Gade."

It is indicative of the groping stage at

which Grieg's genius still paused that he actually tried to write a symphony, two movements
of which are preserved in the Symphonic Pieces,
opus 14—Grieg, whose talent was symphonic
in about the degree that Brahms's was operatic.
Contact with the friendly little man in the large
gray hat, who has been dubbed the " Danish
Mendelssohn," was doubtless a stimulus to the
young Grieg; but other and more radical influences were needed to awaken his personality
and bring him to his own.   Such influences,
however, he actually found in Copenhagen.
The " Nordraak " for whom Gade had at first
taken him, a fervently patriotic Norwegian of
magnetic personality, acquainted him with
Norwegian folk-songs and fired him with an
ambition to found on them a finished art.
Meeting in solemn conclave, with all the self-
importance of youth, these two enthusiasts
took the oath of musical allegiance to their
fatherland.   " It was as though scales fell from
my eyes," writes Grieg; " for the first time I
learned . . . to understand my own nature.
We abjured the Gade - Mendelssohn insipid
and diluted Scandinavianism, and bound ourselves with enthusiasm to the new path which

the northern school is now following." Nor
did their zeal confine itself to composition.
In 1864 they founded, with their Danish friends
Horneman and Matthison-Hansen, the Euterpe
Musical Society, for the performance of Scan-
dinavian works. This institution, which must
have reacted stimulatingly on their composition, they supported energetically up to Grieg's
departure in 1866 for Christiania. Finally, it
was in these years of his freshest vigor, in which
he was conscious both of inner power and of
outer opportunities, that Grieg met the lady,
Miss Nina Hagerup, his cousin, who became in
time his wife. It is not to be wondered at that
no period in his life was so fruitful as this.

His most characteristic works, accordingly,
were composed between his graduation from the
conservatory and the early seventies—between
his twentieth and his thirtieth years. There are
the two inimitable Sonatas for Violin and Piano,
opus 8 and 13; the Piano Sonata, opus 7; the
incidental music to Ibsen's Peer Gynt; some of
the most charming of the Lyric Pieces for piano
and of the Songs, and the Piano Concerto, opus
16; the best part, certainly, of his entire musical product. It were a hopeless as well as use-

less task to describe in words the qualities of these compositions. What shall one say in words of the flavor of an orange? It is sweet? Yes. And acid? Yes, a little. And it has a delicate aroma, and is juicy and cool. But how much idea of an orange has one conveyed then? And similarly with this indescribably delicate music of Grieg ; there is little that can be pertinently or serviceably said of it. One may point out, however, its persistently lyrical character. It is like the poetry of Mr. Henley in its exclusive concern with moods, with personal emotions of the subtlest, most elusive sort. It is intimate, suggestive, intangible. It voices the gentlest feelings of the heart, or summons up the airiest visions of the imagination. It is whimsical, too, changes its hues like the chameleon, and often surprises us with a sudden flight to some unexpected shade of expression. Again, its finesse is striking. The phrases are polished like gems, the melodies charm us with their perfect proportions, the cadences are as consummate as they are novel. Then, again, the rhythm is most delightfully frank and straightforward ; there is no maundering or uncertainty, but always a vigorous dancing progress, as candid as childhood. It is hard to keep one's feet still through some of the Norwegian Dances. And though in the Lyric Pieces rhythm is idealized, it is always definite and clear, so that they are at the opposite pole from all that formless sentimentality which abandons accent in order to wail. Again, we must notice the curious exotic flavor of this music, a flavor not Oriental but northern, a half-wild, half-tender pathos, outlandish a little, but not turgid—on the contrary, perfectly pellucid. An example is a little waltz that figures as number two of the Lyric Pieces, opus 12. Grieg's music, then, is lyrical, intimate, shapely, and exotic, if such words mean anything—yes, just as the orange is sweet, acid, and aromatic. One who would feel the quality of these works must hear them.

On the other hand, Grieg is never large or heroic; he never wears the buskin. He has neither the depth of passion nor the intellectual grasp needed to make music in the grand style. Probably of all his peculiarities the most significant is the shortness of his phrases and his manner of repeating them almost literally, displaced a little in pitch, but not otherwise altered. Almost all his music can be cut up into segments two or four measures long, each segment complete in itself, an entire musical thought. If the reader will examine the little Waltz just mentioned, for example, he will see that it is constructed as follows: after two introductory measures a phrase of melody is announced, four measures in length; this is immediately repeated, at the same pitch but slightly varied in rhythm; then enters another phrase, two measures long, which is repeated literally a third lower; its latter half is twice echoed, and there is a two-measure cadence. All is then repeated. The middle part of the piece, in A major, is built in much the same way; after it the first part is given once more, and there is a short coda. The construction of this charming piece, in a word, is very like that of the passages from primers that are familiar to us all: " Is this a boy? This is a boy. Has the boy a dog? The boy has a dog. This is the dog of the boy." And Grieg's coda adds meditatively, "Of the boy . . . . the boy . . . . boy." His thoughts complete themselves quickly; they have little span, and they are combined, not by interfusion, but by juxtaposition. He never weaves a tapestry; he assembles a mosaic. We have only to compare his music with that of some great master, of wide scope and large synthetic power, like Brahms or Beethoven, to feel precisely in what sense he is lyrical rather than heroic, charming rather than elevated, suggestive rather than informative. Compare, for instance, with his waltz, the waltz of Brahms, number eight in opus 39. Here there is a sustained flight of twelve measures, the tune poising and soaring as it were on a rising or falling breeze, or like a kite that now dips and now is up again, but never touches the earth. It is interesting to play the two waltzes one after the other, noting the difference in effect between the precise, dainty, clipped phrases of the one and the broad-spanned arch of melody of the other. Such contrasts are at the basis of all significant discriminations of musical form.

How much the "short breath" of Grieg is due to the nature of his thematic material is a difficult question to answer. Folk-tunes, it is certain, are simple in structure, composed of short phrases expressing the naïve emotions of childlike minds. On the other hand, had they not fulfilled Grieg's personal needs, supplying the sort of atmosphere he was meant to breathe in, he could never have assimilated them as he has done. Perhaps a true account of the matter is that his nature is of such unusual simplicity and ingenuousness as to find in folk-melodies its natural utterance, and to feel in their primitive phrase-structure no limitation. Intellectually, the man is not more mature than the people. From whatever sources he might draw his germinal ideas, he would never combine them in complexer forms or larger patterns than he has found ready-made to his hand in the national song. There are, however, in Norwegian music peculiarities of a different sort that we can hardly conceive as proving other than hindrances in the formation of a wholesomely eclectic style — peculiarities which are all present full-fledged in so early a work of Grieg as the Piano Concerto, opus 16, written in 1868. At the very outset, in the descending octave passage, there are two melodic tricks that recur everywhere in Grieg—the fall from the seventh of the scale to the fifth, and from the third to the tonic. Both progressions, anomalous in classic music, are prominent features of the Northern folk-tunes. Then, in the first theme, assigned to the orchestra, there are to be noticed, besides these melodic steps, the bodily displacement of the phrase already described, carrying it from A minor into C major. In the second theme, as well as in the *cantabile* piano passage that prepares the way for it, there is a rhythmic device characteristic of Grieg— the mixing in one measure of three notes to the beat with two notes to the beat, of which the prototype is to be found in the " Springtanz " of Norwegian peasants. Here also is the weak cadence, that is to say, the cadence with tonic chord coming on an unaccented beat. So much for melodic and rhythmic peculiarities; as a harmonist Grieg has methods equally persistent. His love of bare fifths, reiterated in the bass with boorish vigor, and his manner of harmonizing with descending chromatic sixths or thirds, both of which we remarked in opus 3, are illustrated in this Concerto; the first in the conclusion-theme of the first movement, and the second in measures fourteen to sixteen of the beautiful Adagio. Finally, he is devoted to the secondary sevenths, especially in harsh and daring sequence such as make up most of the Norwegian March, opus 54, No. 2. Mannerisms like these Grieg has, on the whole, in far larger measure than most composers. On almost any of his pages the student will have no difficulty in finding for himself instances of one or more of these mannerisms.

Now, so many little tricks and idiosyncrasies, however piquant in the work of a beginner, could hardly escape becoming, as time went on, an incubus to even the most vigorous imagination. Nothing menaces thought more than affectations and whimsicalities of style. And even in the meridian of Grieg's activity, when he was charming a staid world with the fresh beauties of the Piano Sonata and the two early Violin Sonatas, there were not wanting critics who discerned his danger and foresaw that he must either broaden his methods or deteriorate. Over twenty years ago the following words were written in an English magazine by Frederick Niecks: " My fear in the case of Grieg always was that his love of Norwegian idioms would tend to narrow, materialize, and make shallow his conceptions, and prevent him from forming a style by imposing on him a manner." Subsequent events have proved that this fear was but too well founded. Although, during the years at Copenhagen, and the eight years, from

1866 to 1874, that Grieg lived in Christiania teaching and conducting, he continued to do excellent work, he seems to have even then reached the acme of his powers, and thenceforward to have imperceptibly declined. It is rather a melancholy fact that when, in 1874, receiving a pension of sixteen hundred crowns from the Government, which enabled him to resign the conductorship of the Musical Union of Christiania, he began to devote himself almost entirely to composition, his mental vivacity was waning and his lovely lyrical utterance was beginning to be smothered under mannerisms. From this time on he advanced more by familiarizing the world with his earlier compositions than by adding to them anything particularly novel or precious. He traveled in Germany, Holland and Denmark, gave concerts in England in 1888, and visited France a year later, playing and conducting his works at Paris. For the rest, he retired to his picturesque villa, Troldhangen, ten miles from Bergen, where he lives a peaceful and secluded country life.

It is not difficult to see why Grieg's later works should decline rather than advance. In the first place, his interest had been from the

first concentrated on personal expression. His
impulse was individual, not universal. He
never sought to widen or deepen the forms of
musical beauty, to extend the range of resources
at the command of musicians; he merely used
what he found ready-made to voice his own poetic feeling. In this he succeeded admirably.
In the second place, charmed by the exotic
quality of Norwegian music, a quality that he
found also in his own nature, he adopted the
native idiom with eagerness, and spent the years
most composers devote to learning the musical
language in acquiring—a dialect. Thirdly, his
mind was of the type which cares much for
beauty of ornament—even more, perhaps, than
for a highly wrought harmony of line and form.
It was the inevitable result of these three circumstances that, first, he should reach his highest activity in early youth, when romantic feeling is at its acme and thought habitually subjective, and thereafter decline; second, that the
dialect which at first was so charming, with its
unfamiliar words and its bewitching accent,
should eventually reveal its paucity and its pro-
vincialism; and finally, that a mind naturally
fond of rich detail, neglectful of large shapeli-

ness, should have recourse, in the ebb of inner
impulse, to transcription, paraphrase, and all
the other devices for securing superficial ornament and luxury of effect. With opus 41 Grieg
began transcribing his own songs for the piano,
dressing up the simple melodies in all sorts of
arpeggios, curious harmonies, and other musical decorations ; and between his fiftieth and
seventieth opus-numbers there is little but representation of Norwegian tunes, now in one
guise and now in another, but seldom indeed
with any of the old novel charm. (A trace of
it there is, perhaps, in opus 62, No. 2, and again
in opus 80, No. 4.) The extraordinary pyro-
technical display that the transcription, opus 41,
No. 5, makes out of so simple a song as "The
Princess" is branded by M. Closson as "un
crime de lèse-art." And to one who has felt
the magic of the Kuhreigen, opus 17, No. 22,
it is saddening to turn to the same melody
as it appears in opus 63, No. 2, with all its
maiden grace brushed and laced and furbelowed
into an *à la mode* elegance and vacuity. Thus
Grieg has not, like the more cosmopolitan, objective, and universal composers, advanced in
his work up to the very end. As years have

progressed, the accidental in it, the inessential, has become more prominent, has tended to obscure what is vital and beautiful. As the spirit waned, the letter has become more rigidly insistent. Idiosyncrasy has supplanted originality. To find the true Grieg, supple, spontaneous, and unaffected, we must go back to the early works.

When all is said, however, Grieg has in these early works made a contribution to music which our sense of his later shortcomings must not make us forget. His Piano Sonata and his Violin Sonatas supply chamber-music with a note of pure lyric enthusiasm, of fresh unthinking animation, not elsewhere to be found. His Peer Gynt Suite fills a similar place among orchestral works. His best piano pieces, and, above all, his lovely and too little known songs, are unique in their delicate voicing of the tenderest, most elusive personal feeling, as well as in their consummate finesse of workmanship. It is a Lilliputian world, if you will, but a fair one. That art of the future which Grieg predicts in his essay on Mozart, which "will unite lines and colors in marriage, and show that it has its roots in all the past, that it draws susten-

ance from old as well as from new masters,"
will acknowledge in Grieg himself the source
of one indispensable element—the element of
naïve and spontaneous romance.

BIBLIOGRAPHICAL NOTE.—Grieg has had the good sense to
publish almost all of his works in the inexpensive and excellent
Peters Edition. The amateur will wish to acquaint himself first
of all with some such representative pieces as the following:
Piano-pieces—Poetic tone-pictures, op. 3, Humoreskes, op. 6,
Sonata, op. 7, Northern Dances, op. 17, Albumblatter, op. 28,
and the Lyric Pieces, op. 12, 38, 43, and 47 (op. 54, 57, 62,
65, and 68 are inferior). Four hand arrangements—Elegiac
Melodies, op. 34, Norwegian Dances, op. 35, and the first
Peer Gynt Suite, op. 40. Chamber-music—the three Sonatas
for Violin and Piano and the 'Cello Sonata, op. 36. Of the
songs, sixty are printed in the five "Albums" of the Peters
Edition. The second contains half a dozen of Grieg's most
perfect songs, among them "I Love Thee," "Morning
Dew," "Parting" and "Wood Wanderings." "To Spring-
time" in Album I, "A Swan" and "Solvejg's Song" in
Album III, and "By the Riverside," "The Old Mother,"
and "On the Way Home" in Album IV, are also characteristic and beautiful. The reader who feels Grieg's charm at all
will end by buying all five Albums, though there is little of
value in the last.

III
ANTONIN DVOŘÁK

ANTONIN DVOŘÁK

III
ANTONIN DVOŘÁK

O N an October evening in 1892 there was given in New York City a " Grand Concert " in exploitation of the " Eminent Composer and Director of the National Conservatory of Music of America," Dr. Antonin Dvořák. There was an orchestra of eighty, a chorus of three hundred, and an audience of several thousand ; the ceremonies, partly hospitable and partly patriotic, included an oration, the presentation of a silver wreath, and the singing of " America " by the assembled multitude. Outwardly picturesque as the occasion doubtless was, it must have been even more striking in its suggestion of the extreme contrasts in life which accompany the turning of fortune's wheel. Here was a man, originally a

Bohemian peasant, a village butcher's son, who for years had endured the most grinding poverty, the most monotonous obscurity, the most interminable labor for power and recognition, coming at last, a famous musician, to hear his works performed and his genius extolled in a great, enthusiastic country that wanted, and was " willing to pay for," a school of music. Even statistics are eloquent when character is behind them ; at a salary of fifteen thousand dollars a year the National Conservatory of America had engaged as principal the composer who, less than twenty years before, had been pensioned by the Austrian Ministry of Education just one hundredth of that sum. Dvořák's reception in New York was an appropriate outward sign of a victory achieved over peculiarly indifferent destiny by peculiarly indomitable pluck.

As one looks back from this imposing event over the course of Dvořák's laborious, persistent youth, one's attention, no matter how much it is at first engaged with the changes of his outer life, with his progress from obscure poverty to comfort and fame, soon dwells even more on the underlying identity of the man through all changes, on his unswerving simplicity of na-

ture and steadfastness of aim. More remarkable than the diversity of his career is the unity
of his character. From first to last, whether in
Mühlhausen, Prague, London, or New York,
he is essentially a peasant. His deepest moral
trait is the dumb persistence, the unthinking
doggedness, of the peasant. His mental atmosphere is the peasant's innocence of self-con-
sciousness, his unintrospective candor. Not
like the sophisticated man, who weighs motives
and foresees obstacles, does he pursue his troub-
lous way. He is, on the contrary, like an en-
gine placed on the track and started; through
darkness and day, through failure and success,
through weakness and strength, he steams ahead,
ever propelled by irresistible inner force, insensible and unamenable to circumstance. And
his musical impulse is of the same sort. His
aims in music have always been simple, definite,
unsophisticated by intellectualism. Taking keen
delight in the sensuous beauty of sound, gifted
with the musical sense in its most fundamental
form of physical susceptibility, from his earliest
days he set about learning to produce pleasant
effects of rhythm and consonance, with utter
sincerity, with no reference to derivative and

secondary musical values. When, as a boy, he heard the villagers playing their native dances, his blood stirred in sympathy, and as soon as he was able he took a hand. When he was older he invented similar pieces, gradually refining them, but always cherishing the brightness of tone, the vigor of rhythmic life, that had first won his devotion. And when, in New York, an experienced and honored musician, he was expected to advise our composers, it was highly characteristic of him that he recommended them to pour their ideas into the negro molds. Here was a music simple, sensuous, highly rhythmic; he looked no further, he was disconcerted by no ethnological problems, nor even by the incongruity that any man of the world would have seen between negro song and our subtly mingled, highly complex American character. Bohemian folk-melodies had expressed him; why should not plantation tunes express us? But perhaps his curious simplicity reveals itself most of all in his perfectly uncritical fecundity as a composer. He writes with extreme rapidity, and indefatigably. The great Stabat Mater is said to have been completed in six weeks, and his opus numbers extend beyond a hundred. He writes as if nothing existed in the world but himself and an orchestra waiting to play his scores. He is never embarrassed by a sense of limitation, by the perception in others of powers he lacks. Though he has studied the masters, he is not abashed by them. The standards of scholarship, those academic bugbears, have for him no terrors. Indeed, of all great composers he is perhaps least the scholar, most the sublimated troubadour, enriching the world with an apotheosized tavern-music. In reading his life we must never forget these things : his simple nature, his sensuous rather than emotional or intellectual devotion to music, and his immunity from the checks and palsies of wide learning and fastidious taste.

There is in a rural district of Bohemia, on the Moldau River, a quiet little village called Nelahozeves, or, in German, Mühlhausen,* where, in 1841, was born Antonin, eldest son of Frantisek Dvořák, the village innkeeper and butcher. The Dvořáks were people not without consideration among their fellow-townsmen ; not

* A graphic picture of the sleepy little place is given in the essay on Dvořák in " Studies in Modern Music," W. H. Hadow, Second Series. Macmillan, New York, 1894.

only was mine host of the tavern a widely acquainted man, but his wife's father was bailiff
to a prince.   One may imagine the potency, in
a small hamlet, of such a conjunction of prom-
inence and prestige.   Nevertheless, as social
distinction has no direct effect on a man's in-
come, and as the butcher's family grew in the
course of years inconveniently numerous, it
happened that Antonin, the eldest of eight
children, was looked to in early youth to learn
his father's trade and contribute toward the
family support.   Unfortunately, he wished to
be a musician.   Such a desire, indeed, chimerical as it may have appeared at the time, was
natural enough in a boy of musical sensibility
who had been surrounded from his earliest years
by a people passionately devoted to music.
Not only is music a part of the instruction in
the Bohemian public schools, but it is the ad-
junct of all the occasions of life.   As many as
forty dances are said to be practiced by the
peasants, and we have it on Dvořák's own
authority that laborers in Bohemia sing at their
work, and after church on Sunday begin dancing, which they " often keep up without cessa-
tion till early on the following morning."

Taking advantage of his opportunities, the boy had learned at fourteen to play the violin, the organ, and the piano, and to sing. It was a year later that, summoned by his father to surrender his dreams of musicianship, he performed an exploit well worth mentioning, as an early example of his indefatigable persistence and his blundering methods. Hoping to enlist his father's sympathy, he wrote, scored, and had played by the village band, an original polka. Mr. Hadow tells the story at length; its point is that Dvořák, whose ambition was more robust than his learning, failed to write the trumpets as transposing instruments, and, of course, made a distressing fiasco. " There is some little irony in the disaster," comments Mr. Hadow, " if it be remembered that among all Dvořák's gifts the instinct of orchestration is perhaps the most conspicuous. He is the greatest living exponent of the art; and he was once in danger of forfeiting his career through ignorance of its most elementary principle." He did, indeed, give up music for a year, but in October, 1857, was allowed by his father to enter the Organ School at Prague.

Had Dvořák been of an introspective turn
of mind, he might now have wondered rather
dismally, as the months went by in Prague, the
paternal allowance ceased, and the tuition at
the Organ School proved narrow and technical,
whether he had really benefited himself. Fortunately, he was not given to metaphysical
speculation; he got what training he could from
the school and joined a band. In Mühlhausen
he had often taken a viola part in the village
band that played for weddings and on holidays;
now he turned his skill to account in the res-
taurants of Prague. In this way, and by playing also in a church orchestra on Sundays, he
managed to amass about nine dollars a month,
and to acquire an instinct for the way instru-
mental parts should be written. The only obvious advantage of this trying period was the
intimate knowledge of instruments it gave him.
He lived, so to speak, cheek by jowl with them,
watching them, handling them, seeing what was
written for them, and hearing how it sounded.
His is no book-knowledge of orchestration. On
the other hand, his extreme poverty, the limitations of the school, and his lack of friends to
lend him scores or the use of a piano, cut him

off cruelly from that equally essential part of
education, familiarity with classic masterpieces
and the traditions of academic learning. His
band played only popular overtures and the
usual pot-pourris. Sometimes he coaxed a ket-
tle-drummer to let him crouch behind the
drums and hear a concert. He once had an
opportunity to hear " Der Freischütz " for the
modest sum of four cents, but the four cents was
not forthcoming, and " Der Freischütz " went
unheard. He could afford to buy no scores,
and there was no library where he could read
them. Such were the meager advantages of
which he made good use ; such the heavy obstacles he gradually surmounted.

After his graduation from the Organ School
in 1860 his situation, both practical and musical,
slowly ameliorated. From Smetana, who gave
him a position in the orchestra of the Interims-
theater, a home for Bohemian opera founded in
1862, he received what was of even more importance to him, the loan of scores and encourage-
ment in composition. Already twenty-one, he
acquainted himself for the first time with Beethoven's and Mendelssohn's symphonies and
chamber-works, of which he became a passionate

student, and with Schumann's songs. For almost
ten years he labored steadily and silently. It
was the period of apprenticeship, the period of
arduous, slow mastery of technique and thought
through which every creative artist must pass.
The mere mass of his exercises is bewildering ;
he composed and destroyed an opera and two
symphonies, to say nothing of many other
sacrifices on the altar of skill of which not even
the names survive. Peculiar to himself, to be
sure, and scarcely a model for other students,
was his method in this long self-evocation. Not
like Beethoven did he meditate and revise his
themes, spending infinite labor on sixteen bars
of melody, and not quailing before a dozen revi-
sions so they were needed to pare away the
marble and reveal the perfect form. Not like
Brahms did he install a systematic training, day
by day winning strength and plasticity of thought
on the chest-weights and dumb-bells of contrapuntal exercise. On the contrary, he forged
ahead, and somehow, without knowing where
he was going or what he was doing, made himself a master. He took Parnassus by storm,
as it were, overran rather than scaled it, and
was victor more by quantity than by quality of

performance.   Yet in all this blundering progress he was protected by a genuine elevation of
aim.   Lacking the sense of tradition and the
safeguards of scrupulous taste, he was not without his own rugged idealism.   And so, although
he doubtless had every external inducement to
join the ranks of the national movement in
music, then just acquiring momentum, he main-
tained his conscientious silence for nearly a decade.   His compositions saw the light neither
of the concert hall nor of the printing-press;
written with ardor, they were burned without
regret.   Dvořák showed in his *lehrjähre* the
self-respect of all really great artists.

It was early in the seventies that he finally
emerged from his studious reserve and appeared
before the world with an opera, " The King and
the Collier," which he was commissioned to
write for the National Theater.   So clear was
the patriotic intent of this commission, so entirely
was the popular interest enlisted in Smetana's
effort to build up a Bohemian school of music,
that it is hard to conceive how Dvořák could
have fallen into the error he now made.   He
prepared for his fellow-countrymen a Wagnerian music-drama.   The situation is comic.

The good Bohemians, come to hear folk-tunes, were given leit-motifs and "infinite melody." If they failed to sympathize with his adoration for the Bayreuth master (and it seems indeed to have been but a calf-sickness, afterwards bravely outlived), if "The King and the Collier" was a flat failure, Dvořák had no one but himself to blame. At this point, however, as at so many others in his career, his unfailing energy saved the day so nearly lost by what one critic has called his "brainlessness." He set to and rewrote his work entire, leaving not a single number of the unhappy music-drama. But now the libretto, which had at first been spared a disapproval all concentrated upon the music, proved worthless and flat, and the opera was damned afresh. Still Dvořák persisted. Getting a poet to set an entirely new "book" to his entirely new music, he made at last a success with an opera of which Mr. Hadow well says that "the Irishman's knife, which had a new blade and a new handle, does not offer a more bewildering problem of identity." No one but Dvořák would have so bungled his undertaking ; no one but he would so have forced it to a successful issue.

By 1873 Dvořák was well started on the career of increasing power and fame that he had worked so hard to establish on firm foundations. That year was marked not only by his installment as organist at St. Adalbert's Church, with a comfortable salary, and by his marriage, but also by the appearance of a composition which made his name at once widely known in Bohemia—the patriotic hymn entitled " The Heirs of the White Mountain." Four years later his reputation began to spread beyond the border. It was in 1877 that the approbation of Brahms, then a commissioner of the Austrian Ministry of Education, to which Dvořák had submitted some duets, induced Joachim to introduce the young Bohemian's works into England and Germany, and the house of Simrock to publish them. In 1878 the Slavonic Dances made their composer's name immediately known throughout the musical world. His great Stabat Mater, produced in England with acclaim in 1883, was the first of several choral works given there in the next few years, all very successfully. In 1889 he was decorated by the Austrian court. In 1890 he received an Honorary Doctorate from the University of Cambridge, was made Doctor

of Philosophy at Prague, and was appointed
Professor of Composition at the Conservatory
there. The welcome accorded to him in America has already been briefly chronicled. His
sixtieth birthday was celebrated by a musical
festival in 1901, at Prague, where he now makes
his home. In Dvořák's varied life a youth of
unusual hardship, of an almost unparalleled
severity of struggle both for livelihood and for
education, has been crowned with years full of a
prosperity and honor rarely allotted to composers.

That time-honored tool of artistic criticism,
the distinction between thought and expression
—or, as the critics say, between *ethos* and technique—is one that constantly tempts the critic
of music, and always betrays him. Very seductive it is, because analogy with other arts is
so plausible a device for exploiting music; but
push it to its logical outcome and it inevitably
vanishes—the form proves to be not the invest-
iture, nor even the incarnation, of the thought,
but the thought itself. Change the expression
and you annihilate the thought; develop a
technique and you create a system of ideas;
mind and body are ultimately one. Now the

case of Dvořák is strongly corroborative of such a theory of the identity in music of *ethos* and technique. What is seen from one angle of vision as his love of exotic color, his devotion to curious intervals of melody, sudden excursions in tonality, and odd molds of rhythm, appears from the other, the technical side, as mastery of orchestral sonority and inheritance of a peculiar musical dialect. It is therefore difficult to account exactly for the genesis of any given quality in his work. Is it the result of an outer influence acting upon a peculiarly plastic nature, or does it spring rather from deeply-rooted individual traits that have dominated the course of his development and shaped his style? Did his early experiences in a village band, for example, awaken and evolve his sense of tone color, or would his music have been primarily sensuous even if he had had the training of Brahms, Tschaïkowsky, or César Franck? It seems probable that here, as elsewhere, inner endowment and outer influence have reacted with a subtlety and complexity that defy analysis, and thought and style are but aspects of one essence. Consequently, the difference between *ethos* and technique, however serviceable as a means of getting over the ground, as a tool of investigation, will mislead us unless we constantly remember how partial is its validity. We may indeed, for the sake of clearness and thoroughness, speak first of one aspect, then of another, but the man we are studying, like the shield in the allegory, remains all the time one.

To approach the technical side first, there can be no doubt that the rich quality of Dvořák's tone, a quality so striking that Mr. Hadow places him with Beethoven, Berlioz, and Wagner in the class of supreme masters of orchestration, would never have been attainable to one who had not had his peculiar experience. He has the practical player's exhaustive knowledge of instruments, which enables him, by disposing the parts always in effective registers, to get a rich and mellow sonority in his *ensemble* writing. Examine any chord in his scores, and you see that each player gives a tone that he can sound fully and advantageously, and that each choir of instruments—the strings, the wood, the brass—gives in isolation an effective chord. The resultant harmony is a well-balanced, thoroughly fused mass of tone. But far

more important than the power to write effect-
ively disposed single chords is the power to
weave a fabric of close texture and firm con-
sistency, to make the orchestra sustain, ramify,
and reinforce itself, so to speak. By far the
best way to secure this solidity of texture is to
write coherent and well-individualized melodies
in the different parts, which serve as strands to
bind the whole. Such is the method of Beethoven among classic and of Tschaïkowsky
among romantic composers, and so efficient is
good polyphonic or " many-voiced " writing as
a means of sonority that it has been truly said,
" Pure voice-leading is half an orchestra." Yet
great skill is required for such polyphonic writing, since all the independent melodies must
coöperate harmoniously; and Dvořák, who got
little academic training as a boy, is not a great
contrapuntist. Just here, however, his band
experience coming to his aid, he was saved
from writing lumpish, doughy stuff—in which
one poor tune in the soprano vainly attempts
to hold up a heavy weight of amorphous " accompaniment "—by his extraordinary knack of
vitalizing his entire mass of tone through rhythmic individualization of the parts. Taking a

skeleton of simple harmony, he manages to write
for the different voices such salient and individual rhythms that they stand out with almost
the grace of melodious contrapuntal parts. It
is a sort of metrical yeast to keep his bread
from being soggy. Numerous examples will at
once occur to students of his scores, particularly
from the Slavonic Dances and Rhapsodies. A
third form of his orchestral mastery might be
pointed out in the well-calculated special effects
for single instruments, such as the oboe duet
that concludes the first movement of the Suite,
opus 39, which occur everywhere in his scores.
But that is, after all, a commoner form of skill,
whereas rich sonority and life in the fabric as
the result of rhythmic individualization of the
parts, can be found in few scores so highly developed as in those of Dvořák.

As regards structure, Dvořák is felicitous but
eccentric. He does not lay out his plans with
the careful prevision of one to whom balance
and symmetry are vital. His scheme is not
foreordered, it is sketched currently. Thus,
for example, his modulation is singularly radical, impulsive and haphazard. He loves to
descend unexpectedly upon the most remote

keys, never knows where he will turn next, and
when he gets too far from home returns over
fences and through no-thoroughfares.   Often,
with him, a change of key seems dictated merely by a desire for a particular patch of color; he
wishes to brighten the tonal background with
sharps or mollify it with flats, and plump he
comes to his key, little caring how he gets there
or where he is going next.   His use of contrasts
of tonality is thus characteristic of his love of
color-effects for themselves and his willingness
to subordinate to them purity of line.   Again,
it is probably not forcing the point to see in his
use of uneven rhythms, such as five and seven
bar periods, another instance of the same tendency to license.   Undoubtedly in part a
legacy from Bohemian folk-song, which is
particularly rich in them, his uneven rhythms
seem to be also in part due to a certain fortuit-
ousness of mind.   It is as if he closed his
phrase, without regard to strict symmetry,
wherever a good chance offered.   The theme
of the Symphonic Variations, opus 78, is an example.   It is interesting to contrast this rhythmic trait of Dvořák's with Grieg's accurate and
sometimes almost wearisome precision of out-

line. Both men derive from folk-music a love of incisive meter—their music has a strong pulse; but Grieg, who is precise, lyrical, sensitive to perfection of detail, is really finical in his unfaltering devotion to square-cut sections, while Dvořák, more wayward, less perfect and exquisite, strays into all sorts of odd periods. His somewhat arbitrary treatment of tonality relations and of rhythm is thus illustrative of a general laxity of method highly characteristic of the man. In contrast with a jealously accurate artist like Grieg, he is felicitous more by force of genius than by wisdom of intent.

Dvořák's childlike spontaneity is in no way better exemplified than by his attitude toward folk-music, and here again he may profitably be contrasted with Grieg. Both devotees of local color have enriched art with unfamiliar lineaments and unused resources, yet their modes of procedure have been quite different. Grieg, traversing the usual mill of German musical education, turned consciously to Norwegian folk-song to find a note of individuality. Struck with the freshness of the native dances, he transplanted them bodily into his academic flower-pots. His courtship of the national

Muse was conscious, sophisticated, and his style is in a sense the result of excogitation. Dvořák, on the contrary, growing up in his small Bohemian village, unable to get classic scores, assiduously fiddling throughout his youth at village fêtes where the peasants must have a scrap of tune to dance by, became thoroughly saturated with the rude music. It moved in his veins like blood ; it was his other language. Thus the two men were at quite polar standpoints in relation to nationalism. With Dvořák it was a point of departure, with Grieg it was a goal of pilgrimage. And so, while the Norwegian has tended to immure himself in idiosyncrasy, the Bohemian has rubbed off provincialisms without losing his inheritance. His music, while retaining the sensuous plenitude, the individual flavor, the florid coloring, with which his youth endowed it, has acquired, with years and experience, a scope of expression, a maturity of style, and a universality of appeal that make it as justly admired as it is instinctively enjoyed.

Imperceptibly we have passed from technical analysis into personal inventory. And indeed, all Dvořák's peculiarities of style may be viewed as the inevitable manifestations of a nature at once rich and naïve. His music makes a delightfully frank appeal. It is never somber, never crabbed, never even profound. It breathes not passion, but sentiment. It is too happily sensuous to be tragic, too busy with an immediate charm to trouble about a remote meaning. Even when he is moving, as in the Largo of the New World Symphony, is it not with a gentle, half-sensuous pathos, a wistfulness more than half assuaged by the wooing sweetness of the sounds that fill our ears? To him music is primarily sweet sound, and we shall misconceive his aim and service if in looking for something deep in him we miss what is, after all, very accessible and delightful for itself—the simple charm of his combinations of tone.

BIBLIOGRAPHICAL NOTE.—Dvořák's fecundity is surprising. He has written cantatas, oratorios, a mass, a requiem, and hymns for chorus and orchestra; five symphonies, five overtures, four symphonic poems, the well-known Slavonic Dances and Rhapsodies, concertos for piano, violin, and violoncello, the inimitable Suite, op. 39, the Symphonic Variations, op. 78, and other orchestral works of smaller proportions; seven string quartets, a sextet, three trios, a terzetto for two violins and a viola, two string quintets, a piano quintet, a piano quartet, a sonata for violin and piano, and a serenade for wind instruments; and, finally, many piano works and songs. He is at his best in his orchestral

and chamber works, of which the following are typical : the
Slavonic Dances, op. 46 and 72, the Slavonic Rhapsodies, op.
45, the Suite, op. 59, the Symphony, " From the New World,"
op. 95, and the Scherzo Capriccioso, op. 66 ; the Sextet, op.
48, the Quartet and Quintet on negro themes, op. 96 and 97,
the Piano Quintet, op. 81, and the Piano Quintet, op. 87.
Though these compositions lose much in transcription, they are
all obtainable in four-hand piano arrangements. The piano
music is somewhat unidiomatic except the later things, but the
Mazurkas, op. 56, the Poetische Stimmungsbilder, op. 85, and
the Humoreskes, op. 101, are worth knowing. Of the songs,
nine of the best are published separately by the house of Simrock, and the two most popular ones, " Gute Nacht " and
" Als die Alte Mutter," are to be had in Schirmer's series entitled " Gems of German Songs." A study of these will probably arouse a desire for more, and the student may buy the Gipsy
Songs, op. 55, and the Love Songs, op. 83. The duets,
" Klänge aus Mähren," not very well known, are characteristic.

IV
CAMILLE SAINT-SAËNS

CAMILLE SAINT-SAËNS

IV
CAMILLE SAINT-SAËNS

*

IT is a principle of musical expression that of the two great types of temperament, the active and the contemplative, the first tends to express itself in strongly rhythmic figures, the second in phrases of vaguer outline, full of sentiment not easily to be confined in molds. The man of action is incisive, vigorous, compact in utterance; the mystic is by contrast indefinite and discursive. It has been well established, indeed, that primeval music was the product of two modes of instinctive emotional expression, the gesticulatory and the vocal, dance and song; and throughout its growth these two strands, however closely they may intertwine, can still be traced. Thus it happens that even to-day we find the complex work of

modern musicians getting a special impress of
personality and style according as the rhythmic
or the melodic-harmonic faculty predominates
in the individual. One man's music will be
notable for its strong impulse, its variety and
vivacity of rhythm ; another's will appeal to the
more dreamy and sentimental part of our
natures, will speak to our hearts so movingly
that we shall recognize its descent from the
song rather than from the dance. And in all
such cases the first man will be of the active
temperament, a man of the world, of many interests and great nervous force ; the second
will be contemplative, inclined to the monastic
life, and of great heart rather than keen intelligence.

Such an antithesis of artistic product and of
personal character exists in a peculiar degree
between Camille Saint-Saëns and César Franck,
the two greatest composers France has produced since Bizet. Each of these men is great
by virtue of qualities somewhat wanting in the
other. The one is clever, worldly, learned—
and a little superficial ; the other, profound, religious, of singularly pure and exalted spirit, is
yet emotional to the verge of abnormality. And

so with their music; that of Saint-Saëns is
energetic, lucid, consummately wrought, while
Franck's, more moving and more subtle, is
so surcharged with feeling as to become vague
and inarticulate. A review of their lives and a
brief analysis of their work will bring out more
clearly this divergence of nature, which, in spite
of the many traits they have in common, has
determined them to very different careers and
exacted of them very dissimilar artistic services.

At a concert given in Paris in 1846 appeared
a new prodigy, a boy pianist, "le petit Saint-
Saëns," as the "Gazette Musicale" announced
him, who, only ten and a half years old, played
Händel, Bach, Beethoven, and Mozart, "without notes, with no effort, giving his phrases
with clearness, elegance, and even expression
in the midst of the powerful effects of a numerous orchestra using all its resources." This,
the first public appearance of Saint-Saëns, was
by no means his first musical exploit. We read
that he began the study of the piano with his
great-aunt at the age of three, when already his
sense of tone was so keen that he would press
down with his left hand the slender fingers of
the right until they became strong enough to

satisfy his exacting requirements; that at five he composed little waltzes; that at ten he played fugues by Bach, a concerto of Hummel, and Beethoven's C-minor Concerto; and that he could tell the notes of all the clock-chimes in the house, and once remarked that a person in the next room was "walking in trochees." By the time he was seventeen he had earned wide reputation as a pianist, had taken prizes for organ-playing at the conservatory, and had written an ode for chorus, solo, and orchestra, and a symphony. Thus early did he lay the foundations of that skill which in the early seventies, when at Wagner's house he played on the piano the "Siegfried" score, won from von Bülow the remark that, with the exception of Wagner and Liszt, he was the greatest musician living.

The surprising energy and versatility shown at the opening of Saint-Saëns's career have proved, in the course of time, to be the salient traits of his typically Gallic nature. He is, to a remarkable degree, the complete Frenchman. He has all the intellectual vivacity, all the nervous force, the quick wit and worldly polish, even the physical swarthiness and the dry keenness of visage, that we associate with his countrymen. M. Georges Serviéres, in his " La Musique Française Moderne," gives the following excellent description : " Saint-Saëns is of short stature. His head is extremely original, the features characteristic ; a great brow, wide and open, where, between the eyebrows, the energy and the tenacity of the man reveal themselves ; hair habitually cut short, and brownish beard turning gray ; a nose like an eagle's beak, underlined by two deeply marked wrinkles starting from the nostrils, eyes a little prominent, very mobile, very expressive. The familiars of his Mondays, those who knew the artist before injured health and family sorrows had darkened his character, remember that there was about him then a keen animation, a diabolic mischievousness, a railing irony, and an agility in leaping in talk from one subject to another with a sprightliness of fancy that equaled the mobility of his features, which were animated at one and the same moment by the most contrary expressions ; and I could cite as instances of his gay humor many funny anecdotes that he loved to tell, adjusting on his nose the while, with both hands, in a way peculiar to him, his eye-glasses, behind which his eyes sparkled with malice." Some examples of this railing irony of Saint-Saëns are preserved. There is, for instance, a story of an ambitious woman at one of his " Mondays," who fairly browbeat him into accompanying her two daughters in a duet. After enduring as long as he could the torture of their timeless and tuneless performance, he turned to the mother with, " *Which* of your daughters, madam, do you wish me to accompany ? " A man of his wit naturally found himself at home in Paris society, and counted among his friends for years such people as the Princess Pauline Metternich, Mme. Viardot-Garcia, and Meissonier, Tourgenieff, and Dumas. A story told in the " Figaro," of how at Madame Garcia's, where he often played both the organ and the piano, he would pass from improvising " masterly pages " in the contrapuntal style to waltzes for the young people to dance by, illustrates in little that peculiar combination of distinction and gayety, characteristic of Paris, which is the native air of Saint-Saëns.

But this adept metropolitan is also an inveterate nomad. Not content with traveling all

over Europe in his virtuoso tours, he has long
had the habit of wintering in outlandish places
like the Canary Islands. Often he leaves home
without announcing to any one his departure,
or even giving friends his addresses; sometimes without knowing himself where he will
go. The spectacle of distant lands and alien
races has for him an inexhaustible fascination.
In writing of his experiences in England, where
he went in 1893 to receive the doctor's degree from Cambridge, he dwells with gusto on
the procession of dignitaries, at the head of
which, he says, "marched the King of Bahonagar, in a gold turban sparkling with fabulous
gems, a necklace of diamonds at his throat."
"Dare I avow," he adds, "that, as an enemy
of the banalities and the dull tones of our modern garments, I was enchanted with the adven-
ture?" And in his charming little essay,
"Une Traversée de Bretagne," the same enthusiasm throws about his oboe-playing ship-cap-
tain the glamour of romance. On his first trip
to the Canaries, made incognito, he is said to
have offered himself as a substitute to sing a
tenor part in "Le Trouvére," and to have
come near appearing in this incongruous rôle.

When his grand opera, "Ascanio," was produced at Paris, he scandalized his friends and
the public by being absent from the first performance. Diligent inquiry, and even the
efforts of the diplomatic agents of the Government, failed to discover his whereabouts, and it
was actually rumored that he had died in Cey-
lon, on his way to Japan. But all the while he
was happily basking in the sun at Palma, scrib-
bling verses. Finally his fondness for astron-
omy is well known, and he is said to have a
private observatory in some "ultimate island."
There is much about this picturesque Frenchman that reminds one of the heroes of Jules
Verne's romances.

When he is at home, Saint-Saëns carries on
a many-sided activity of which composition is
hardly more than half. For one thing, he
is indefatigable in his efforts to improve
public taste. In 1864 he gave in a series of
concerts all the concertos of Mozart; in 1878,
such is the catholicity of his taste, he organized
concerts to produce Liszt's Symphonic Poems.
He has done much for musical bibliography
by his careful editions of Gluck, Rameau, and
others. In 1871 he took active measures to

better the opportunities of young native composers. At that time, as he puts it, "the name of a composer at once French and living, upon a programme, had the property to put everybody to flight." The great improvement that has taken place since then is due largely to him and his brother-workers of the National Society of Music.

His two volumes of critical essays, " Harmonie et Mélodie" and " Portraits et Souvenirs," are marked by soundness of principle, broad eclecticism of taste, and a pungent, epigrammatic style. In general temper he is classical without being pedantic ; that is to say, he has no superstitious awe for rules, but a profound reverence for law. The licenses of modern technique and the mental vagueness of which they are the reflection find in him a formidable foe. The thrust he gives, in the preface of " Portraits et Souvenirs," to those amateurs who are " annoyed or disdainful if the instruments of the orchestra do not run in all directions, like poisoned rats," is typical of his attitude and method. He is a master of innuendo and delicate sarcasm, which he always employs, however, to protect art against affectation and ignorance. In dealing with the theory that music depends for its effect on physical pleasure, he speaks derisively of the solo voice which one can "savor at one's leisure, like a sherbet." He says of those orchestral conductors and choirmasters who always complain of difficulties that they "love above all their little habits and the calm of their existence." Among these sparkling sentences one comes frequently also upon pieces of wisdom, sometimes expressed with rare dignity, as when he writes, " There is in music something which traverses the ear as a door, the reason as a vestibule, and which goes yet further." A writer so highly gifted with both raillery and eloquence might do mischief were he narrow or intolerant. That Saint-Saëns is neither can be seen from a mere enumeration of some of his subjects, chosen almost at random: there are essays on The Oratorios of Bach and Händel, Jacques Offenbach, Liszt, Poetry and Music, The Nibelungen Ring and the Performances at Bayreuth, Don Giovanni, A Defense of Opéra-Comique, The Multiple Resonance of Clocks, and The Wagnerian Illusion.

These titles indicate a wide enough range of

interest, but Saint-Saëns is furthermore a writer on subjects entirely unconnected with music. His devotion to philosophy has prompted him to publish a volume called " Problèmes et Mystéres ; " an antiquarian interest has found expression in his " Note sur les décors de Thé-âtre dans l'antiquité romaine ; " and he has printed a volume of poems under the title " Rimes familières." Finally, a comedy in one act called " La Crampe des écrivains " (a dis-ease from which he appears never to have suf-fered) has been successfully produced at Paris.

As a composer, Saint-Saëns impresses the student first of all by his excessive, his almost inordinate, cleverness. It is not seemly for a human being to be so clever; there is some-thing necromantic about it. Look at the open-ing of the G-minor Piano Concerto and see a modern Frenchman writing like the great Bach. See, in the " Danse Macabre," Berlioz and Johann Strauss amalgamated. Listen to the rich effects of tone in the 'Cello Sonata in C minor. Study the thematic transformations and the contrapuntal style of the Symphony in the same key. Admire the lightness, the cob-web iridescence, of the " Rouet d'Omphale."

The author of these works is obviously a man of great intellectual skill and versatility.

Looking more closely, one observes a duality of style, for the moment puzzling, which properly understood only emphasizes the peculiarity of his artistic impulse. His compositions are of two well-marked varieties which at first seem to have little in common. To begin with, all those cast in the conventional symphonic mold—the three symphonies, the eight concertos, three for violin and five for piano, and most of the chamber-music—are severely, at times almost aridly, classical in conception and execution. They are " absolute music " of the most unequivocal sort. They depend for their effect on clear form, well-calculated symmetry, traditional though interesting melodic and harmonic treatment; their themes are of the family of Haydn and Mozart; their structure is that perfected by Beethoven; their orchestration is skillful but unobtrusive, a transparent medium rather than a rich material garment. In a word, they are very pure examples in music of a type of art—the French classic or pseudo-classic type—which gains little from richness of material or variety of suggestion, which depends for its appeal on clarity and symmetry of form and on clean workmanship in style. But, in addition to these conventional works, Saint-Saëns has produced a whole museum of exotics, in which his aim is to delineate passions, peoples, and places. There are the four Symphonic Poems, for example, the " Rouet d'Omphale," " Phaéton," the " Danse Macabre," and " La Jeunesse d'Hercule," in which he assumes the rôle of story-teller. In the " Nuit à Lisbonne," the " Jota Aragonese," and the " Rapsodie d'Auvergne," he makes a tour in southern Europe; in the " Suite Algerienne " he portrays the deserts about Algiers, and in his opus 89 he gives us a fantasy of odd rhythms and outlandish tonalities supposed to introduce us to Africa. Nothing could seem, at the first blush, more diametrically opposite to the pseudo-classic works than these exotics, which among their academic brothers recall the King of Bahonagar at Cambridge. Yet both kinds, after all, when one looks more closely, are products of the widely questing intelligence, whose interests are dramatic rather than personal. They have this in common, that neither is of primarily emotional origin, that both are

expressions of a mind objective and alertly ob-
servant. The difference between them is that
in the one case this observation takes for object
the purely musical world of tones, and in the
other nature's world of persons, nations, races,
and climates. But whether he is seeking a
piquant rhythm or a curious turn of harmony,
or sketching his impression of Spain or Egypt,
Saint-Saëns is always the onlooker, the man of
the world, never the mystic who contemplates
in his own heart the forces that underlie the
universe.

Strong testimony from the man himself to the
truth of this view is indirectly afforded by
his essay on Liszt, an essay which is furthermore noteworthy as containing in half a dozen
sentences the essential truths of that vexed
question of programme-music. He is, to begin
with, as assertive as we should expect of the
necessity, in all music, of absolute beauty. " Is
the music itself," he says, " good or bad? All
is there. Whether or no it has a programme,
it will not be, for that, better or worse." Thus
far speaks the author of the symphonies, the
concertos, and the chamber-works. The composer of the symphonic poems and the geo-

graphical pieces continues: "But how much greater is the charm when to the purely musical pleasure is added that of the imagination coursing without hesitation over a determined path. . . . All the faculties of the soul are put in play at once, and toward the same end. I can see well what art gains from this, I cannot see what it loses." Here speaks, recognizably enough, the Frenchman. In that phrase about "the imagination coursing without hesitation over a determined path" stands clearly revealed the dramatic point of view characteristic of French art, which is always devoted to the spectacle of life rather than to the elemental passions which underlie it. The satisfactions Saint-Saëns finds in music are those of the formal musical sense and of "the imagination coursing a determined path;" of the emotional satisfaction which music gives so generously he has nothing to say. To take another instance, how admirably logical and how adequate to the composition, which for all its picturesque grace leaves one cold, is the "programme" he appends to the "Rouet d'Omphale." "The subject of this symphonic poem," he writes," is feminine seduction, the triumph of weakness over strength. The spinning-wheel is but a pretext, chosen solely with a view to the rhythm and the general effect of the piece. Those interested in the study of details will see at page 19, Hercules groaning under the bonds he cannot break, and at page 32 Omphale laughing at the vain efforts of the hero." Both programme and piece are the creations of a keen intelligence which records its observations with accuracy and skill, but makes no personal revelation, cares not to contemplate itself, and is moved by no deep and perhaps vague, but nevertheless creative, emotion.

Lack of emotion, then, is the serious defect of this master. And in a musician it is in truth serious. Emotion is the life blood of the musical organism ; without it all the members may be shapely, well ordered, highly finished, but all will be cold and lifeless. So it is with much of this clever craftsman's work. Too often there is graceful melody, arresting harmony, ingenious rhythm, but none of the passion needed to fuse and transfigure them. Impassioned vocal utterance, the song element in music, is seldom heard from Saint-Saëns. In the classic works he manipulates, in the exotic pieces he depicts; nowhere does he speak. But to speak, to voice deep feeling directly, though with the restraint necessary to plastic beauty, is the aim and the justification of music. Complex as the art has become in our day, the essence of it is still, as it ever must be, emotional expression; and though modern composers sing broader songs than the first musicians, and sing them on instruments rather than with the voice, they must equally sing, and their song must proceed from their hearts if it is to touch the hearts of others. Hence Saint-Saëns, when compared with a man of passionate earnestness like César Franck, or Schumann, or Wagner, inevitably seems superficial. Pieces like his B-minor Violin Concerto, with its elaborate classical machinery, its well-planned contrasts and brilliant effects, and the vast Symphony in C-minor, in which the theme undergoes such wonderfully skillful manipulation, seem so little the expression of a personal impulse that we catch ourselves wondering why he wrote them. Elsewhere, to be sure, as in the Andante of the 'Cello Sonata, his very virtuosity achieves such noble effects that we forget the hand-made quality of the work. But it

is seldom indeed that, subordinating workmanship entirely, he gives us a genuine song of
feeling, such as the second theme of the Finale
in this Sonata. The lift and impetus of this
beautiful theme emphasizes by contrast the
emotional emptiness of the ingenious web that
surrounds it.

While, however, we may with propriety recognize the lack of personal ardor in Saint-Saëns
that reduces the song element in his music to a
minimum, it would be a sad mistake to exag-
gerate the limitation or to forget that from another and perhaps an equally valid point of
view he is a great musician. However he may
fall short as a melodist, he is a past-master of
rhythm and harmony, spheres in which feeling
counts for less, logic for more. His harmonic
style is eminently lucid. To him a chord is
part of an organism, not a bit of color or a
phase of feeling. A series of chords has for him
all the tendency, the direction, and the self-ful-
fillment of a sentence of words; to omit or to
change one would be like striking out a predi-
cate or an object—the sentence would not
parse. He uses most those chords which
point in a definite direction, which carry in

themselves, so to speak, the indication for their fulfillment—the dominant and secondary sevenths, and suspensions of triads. He avoids the vague and the ambiguous. And although he is a lover of novel harmonic effects, and an ingenious inventor of them, the novelty is always a new form, not a new formlessness. His modulation, too, is of an extreme clarity: he never falls into a new key, so to speak, as Dvořák does; he proceeds thither.

But even more striking than the clearness of his harmony is the trenchant perspicuity of his rhythm. The sense of rhythm is perhaps the prime criterion of intellectuality in a composer. For just as determinations of accent and measure, such as occur in the dances of the most primeval savages, were undoubtedly the earliest means of formulating the cries and wails of emotion which underlie all musical expression, so throughout musical history rhythm has been the chief formative or rationalizing agent, and a vivid sense of it has always characterized the more intellectual musicians. The dreamers and the sentimentalists are never fastidious of accent; it is the clear, active minds who delight in precise meter. Quite inevitable to a man of

Saint-Saëns's temperament, then, is the instinct for strong, various and subtle rhythms that his compositions reveal at every page. One discerns it in his fondness for pizzicato effects and for the percussion instruments, both of which emphasize the accent. And his devotion to the piano, which he uses more in combination with other instruments than almost any other composer, is doubtless due to the fact that it compensates for its lack of sustained tone by a special incisiveness of attack. Another significant peculiarity is the short groups of repeated notes that occur so often in his writings as to be a mannerism. They are found, for example, in the fourth of his Variations on a Theme of Beethoven, opus 35, in the " scherzando " section of " Africa," at the opening of the Trio, opus 92, in the accompaniment of the well-known air from " Samson et Dalila," " Mon cœur s'ouvre à ta voix," and in the third of the Six Études, opus 52. The effect of this device, which throws a strong emphasis on the first of the reiterated notes, is a peculiar rhythmic salience. Again, on the principle that minor irregularities in a regular plan bring out all the more clearly the larger orderliness, Saint-Saëns loves to alternate groups of four notes with groups of three, or three with two, and to displace his accent entirely by syncopation, which, when properly handled, deepens the ideal stress by setting the actual in competition with it.

In all these and countless other ways are revealed the accuracy and virtuosity of intellect that distinguish this brilliant Frenchman. Clearness of form is, on the whole, so much rarer in modern music than wealth of meaning, that the art in our day has peculiar need of such workers. Their office is to make us remember, in our welter of emotion, the perennial delightfulness of order and control. They are the apologists of reason, without which feeling, however noble, must become futile, inarticulate. In their precise, well-constructed works we find a relief from the dissipating effects of mere passion. We breathe there a serene, if a somewhat rarefied, atmosphere. Of this classic lucidity Saint-Saëns is a great master. However dry he may sometimes be, he is never turgid; however superficial his thought, it is never vague; he offers us his artistic sweets never in the form of syrup —he refines and crystallizes them. If, then, we of a race emotionally profounder and mentally more diffuse find his music sometimes empty for all its skill, we must not for that reason underrate the service he does for music by insisting on articulateness in feeling, logic in development, and punctilious *finesse* in workmanship.

BIBLIOGRAPHICAL NOTE.—Saint-Saëns's best orchestral works are arranged not only for four hands, but for two players at two pianos, a combination of which he is extremely fond. It is interesting to play in this way the four symphonic poems, "La Rouet d'Omphale," "Phaéton," the "Danse Macabre," and "La Jeunesse d'Hercule." The five Piano Concertos are also excellent. The symphonies are rather dry. Of the chamber-music, the 'Cello Sonata, op. 32, and the Violin Sonatas, op. 75 and 102, are particularly good. The piano music is less original, being for the most part pseudo-classic in conception and style. Thus the Suite, op. 90, is like a suite of Bach's with the sincerity taken out. On the whole the Six Études, op. 52, and the Album of six pieces, op. 72, are better worth study. The former contains two able fugues, the latter an odd "Carillon" in 7-4 time and an attractive "Valse." There is charm in "Les Cloches du Soir," op. 85, and also in a well-known melody, without opus-number, called "Le Cygne." Saint-Saëns has little power as a song-writer; those who wish to realize this for themselves, may purchase the Schirmer Album of fifteen of his songs. To his numerous operas no reference is made in the present essay, the subject of which is his contribution to pur · music.

V
CÉSAR FRANCK

CÉSAR FRANCK

V
CÉSAR FRANCK

—

WHEN we turn from the brilliant Parisian we have been studying to that obscure and saintly man, César Franck, the only French contemporary of Saint-Saëns who is worthy to be ranked with him as a great composer, we can hardly believe ourselves in the same country or epoch. It is as if we were suddenly transported from modern Paris into some mediæval monastery, to which the noise of the world never penetrates, where nothing breaks the silence save the songs of worship and the deep note of the organ. In the presence of this devout mystic the sounds of cities and peoples fade away, and we are alone with the soul and God. We have passed from the noonday glare of the intellect, in which objects stand forth sharp and hard, into the soft cathedral twilight of religious emotion; and putting aside our ordinary thoughts we commune for a time with deeper intuitions. Or, again, it is like closing a volume of Taine and taking up Maeterlinck. From the streets and the drawing-room we pass into the cloister, where dwell no longer men and things, but all the intangible presences of thought and feeling. We close our eyes on the pageant of experience, to reopen them in the dim inner light of introspection, where, if we may believe the mystics, they will behold a truer reality. The temperament of Franck is thus at the opposite pole from that prehensile Gallic temperament so well exemplified in Saint-Saëns, and we should find the juxtaposition of the two men as the greatest French composers of their time highly perplexing did we not remember that, in spite of his almost lifelong residence in Paris, César Franck was by birth and blood, like Maeterlinck, with whom he has so much in common, a Belgian. Exactly how much the peculiar characters of these men were inherited from their race it is of course impossible to say; but any one who has seen the placid faces of the Belgian peasants, with their calm, almost bovine look of contentment, must recognize there a trait that needs only the power of articulation to produce a natural religion of feeling, or mysticism, like that of César Franck and Maeterlinck. It was the same sort of self-sufficient serenity, the antithesis of Saint-Saëns's busy worldliness, that determined the course of Franck's life, so obscure, so uneventful, so dominated by high spiritual purpose.

César-Auguste Franck (it was an inapt name for so pacific a being) was born in 1822, at Liége, Belgium. There he made his first musical studies, but went to Paris at fifteen to study in the Conservatory. Though without the precocity of "le petit Saint-Saëns," he must have been a solid musician at sixteen, for in a test that took place in July, 1838, he transposed a piece at sight down a third, playing it "avec un brio remarquable," and was awarded the first grand prize of honor at his graduation in 1842. Foregoing the career of a concert pianist, which his father wished him to pursue, "repudiating with horror and disgust," as one of his biographers has it, "the brilliant noise-making that people long mistook for music," he turned for a livelihood to that laborious work of teaching which he pursued all the rest of his life with patient fidelity.

He seems to have been an almost ideal teacher, long-suffering with the dull pupils, painstaking and generous with the able ones, provoking enthusiasm in all by his contagious love for art and his receptivity to ideas. In a degree that is rare even among the best teachers, he combined endurance and vivacity. Giving, all his life, from eight to ten lessons a day, many of them, even after he had made his reputation, in girls' boarding-schools and *pensions* of the usual wearisome sort, he yet retained vitality to impart to the best minds of the present generation of French composers. Though after teaching all day, often not returning home until supper-time, he would in the evening give correspondence lessons to pupils in the provinces, and though even the Sundays were filled with his duties as organist and choirmaster, still he often found time to assemble his favorite pupils, and to discuss with them, as if with perfect equals, their exercises and his own works. One of these pupils, M. Vincent d'Indy, has described how " père Franck," as they called him, would play them his choral compositions, singing all the vocal parts in "a terrible voice;" and how he would sit at the piano, fixing with troubled gaze some offending passage in an exercise, murmuring anxiously, "Je n'aime pas . . . Je n'aime pas," until perhaps it grew to seem permissible, and with his bright smile he could cry "J'aime!"   Thanks to his earnest desire to appreciate whatever was good, controlled as it was by a severely classical taste, he could make his students good work-men and stern critics without paralyzing their individual genius.   He was thorough without being rigid, and respected learners as much as he revered the masters.   Naturally, the learners, in their turn, felt for their "Pater seraphicus," as they named him, an almost filial affection. Emmanuel Chabrier, speaking over Franck's grave, in Montrouge Cemetery, voiced the feel-ings of them all when he said that this was not merely an admirable artist, but "the dear re-gretted master, the most gentle, modest, and wise.   He was the model, he was the example."

For thirty-two years, that is to say, from 1858 until his death, Franck was organist of the Église Ste. Clothide, where his playing must

have been an endless inspiration to all who
heard him, though his modesty kept him per-
sonally inconspicuous. One likes to think of
this quiet, devout musician, animated by the
purest religious enthusiasm, advancing year by
year in mastery of his art, producing without
ostentation works of a novel and radical beauty.
Few of his listeners could have conceived that
one so benignant and courteous, but so easily
forgotten, was making himself a force that
modern music could not forget. They, who
saw only the husk of the man, could not guess
what treasures of humanity and genius it con-
cealed. M. d'Indy well describes the two
aspects. "Any one," he says, "who had en-
countered this being in the street, with his coat
too large, his trousers too short, his grimacing
and preoccupied face framed in his somewhat
gray whiskers, would not have believed in the
transformation that took place when, at the
piano, he explained and commented on some
beautiful work of art, or when, at the organ, he
put forth his inspired improvisations. Then
the music enveloped him like an aureole; then
one could not fail to be struck by the conscious
will expressed in the mouth and chin, by the

almost superhuman knowledge in his glance; then only would one observe the nearly perfect likeness of his large forehead to that of Beethoven." And M. Derepas has the following paragraph in the same tenor: "It was there, before the keyboards, his agile and powerful feet upon the pedals, that it was necessary to see César Franck. His beautiful head with its finely developed brow crowned with naturally curling hair, his profound and contemplative expression, his features marked without exaggeration, his full, well-cut mouth breathing health, . . . all wearing the aureole of genius and of faith—it was like a vision of another age in strong contrast with the turbulences of the day." If one is sometimes sorry that Franck had to spend so much time teaching, one cannot, in the face of such descriptions as these, regret the hours he passed in the loft of Ste. Clotilde. Its atmosphere was native to his genius, which was not only religious, but even ecclesiastical. In hearing his "musique cathédralesque," as Saint-Saëns well called it, one can almost see the pillars and arches, the pure candle-flames and the bowed peasants at prayer.

It was in the spare moments of this full life

that Franck found time to write his extraordinary music. Every morning, winter and summer, rising at six, he set aside two hours for what he expressively called "his own work." Then, after breakfast, came the day's teaching, in the course of which he would jot down ideas that occurred to him, recording perhaps eight measures, and turning again to the pupil. In the evenings, when there were not correspondence-lessons to write, or rehearsals, he often got out his manuscripts once more; and his short summer vacations were given entirely to composition. All the more remarkable is this indomitability when we remember that he lacked not only the stimulus of public success, but for a long while even the impetus of having definitely succeeded in his own eyes, so new were his ideas and so difficult the technique they required. Very few composers have matured so late. Though he wrote in his youth some trios, and later a Mass, his first really individual work, "Ruth," was written when he was nearly fifty; "Les Éolides," his earliest orchestral composition, was produced in 1877, when he was fifty-five; "Les Beatitudes," in some respects his masterpiece, was not finished until 1880, though begun more than ten years before ; and all his most characteristic work in pure music, as, for example, the Prelude, Choral, and Fugue and the Prelude, Aria, and Finale for piano, the three wonderful Chorals for organ, the Violin Sonata, the Quartet, the Quintet, and the Symphony, date from the last decade of his life. In a day when every harmony-student itches to give the world a symphony, it is hard to admire too much the artistic self-respect that kept Franck a nonentity for years, to make him at last a master.

Meanwhile, of course, he had to endure neglect. Probably most of his acquaintances shared the impression put into words by a Paris publisher to whom M. Serviéres offered an essay about him. " Oh, monsieur," cried this gentleman, "I remember César Franck perfectly. A man who was always in a hurry, always soberly dressed in black, and who wore his trousers too short ! . . . Organist at Sainte Clotilde. It seems that he was a great musician, little known to the public." Rather harder to explain is the lack of appreciation which in 1880 led those in power at the Conservatory, where Franck was already organ professor, to give the chair of

composition then left vacant, not to him, but to
Léo Delibes, the writer of ballet-music. But
perhaps the most pathetic result of the general
indifference to Franck was that his masterpiece
could never be given a complete performance
during his lifetime. " Les Beatitudes " was first
given entire in 1893, three years after his death.
When he received the Legion of Honor in
1886, he said sorrowfully to a friend, " Yes, my
friend, they honor me—as a Professor." That
is the one repining word of his that is recorded.

It would, however, be a mistake to suppose
that Franck's fellow-men noticed nothing but
his short trousers, or that in his high artistic effort he was entirely without sympathy. Few
men have been more fortunate in their friends.
The love and veneration of his many pupils,
and of such men as Chabrier, Pierné, and Fauré,
made an atmosphere in which his heart expanded
and his ambition grew. One of this group of
admirers tells how they would surround him on
his return to Paris in the autumn, to ask what
he had done, what he had to show. " Vous
verrez, repondait-il "—the French alone can
render the endearing vanity and *naïveté* of his
reply—" vous verrez, repondait-il en prenant

un air mysterieux, vous verrez ; je crois que vous serez content. . . . . J'ai beaucoup travaillé et bien travaillé."] It was a similarly frank and guileless self-satisfaction that made him apparently unaware of the coldness of his audiences, who were generally puzzled or bored. Happy, as M. d'Indy records, in having given his friends the pleasure of hearing him play his own compositions, in spite of the scanty applause he never failed to bow profoundly. Thus untroubled by the indifference of the crowd, surrounded by a few men who gave him their warm and discriminating admiration, and inspired by a genius peculiarly exalted and disinterested, bent on beauty alone, and superior to petty jealousies, César Franck lived his quiet, fruitful, and happy life. He died at Paris in 1890. The last anecdote we have of him tells of his finding strength, four days before his death, to praise the " Samson et Dalila " of Saint-Saëns, then running at the Théâtre Lyrique. " I see him yet," says M. Arthur Coquard, " turning towards me his poor suffering face to say vivaciously and even joyfully, in the vibrant tones that his friends know, ' tres beau, tres beau.' " The words, expressing that pure love of art which animated his whole career, lodge in the mind of one who studies it, together with those other words of his, which none ever had a better right to use, " J'ai beaucoup travaillé et bien travaillé."

It has been necessary to dwell at some length on Franck's life and character because they throw so much light on his music. To an unusual degree it is the expression of himself, full of his peculiar contemplative emotion. The harmonic background is rich, somber, and vague, like the prevailing mood of a religious devotee ; from it constantly emerge phrases of song, phrases of the most poignant aspiration, like passions in a dream, voicing those intense yet elusive feelings which irradiate none but introspective minds. They are like the cries of human lovers in a world of silence and mystery, or, better, they are the cries of a finite soul that yearns for God and finds him not. One feels always in Franck's music the tragedy of the finite and the infinite. Those groping, shifting harmonies, above which the pathetic fragments of melody constantly sound for a moment, somehow irresistibly suggest the great unknown universe in which men's little lives are acted.

All is vague save the momentary feature, and that presses on towards a fulfillment that perpetually eludes it. All shifts and passes, save only that never-ceasing mood of aspiration, that restless striving of the fragment for completion. Spiritual unrest is the characteristic quality of this music—the unrest of a spirit pure and ardent but forever unsatisfied.

Now, it is perhaps not too fantastic to find in the mingled vagueness and poignancy of this music the proper artistic expression of mysticism. So *must* a mystic express himself, For it is characteristic of the mystical temperament to yearn for ideal satisfactions, but to find none in finite forms. Mysticism, in fact, is one of the ways of solving, or perhaps we should say of ignoring, that primal and protean mystery of human life, the conflict between ideal needs and actual facts. Realism meets it by denying the needs and exalting the facts; idealism attempts to mold the real into conformity with the ideal, of course with very partial success. The mystic, too earnest to follow the realistic method, too impatient to endure the plodding progress of idealism, cuts the Gordian knot by discarding the actual altogether. He pronounces it too

inelastic, too constricting, and dispenses with it.
He hugs the ideal to his heart, but can see no
virtue in the real.   Actualities, objects, events,
and forms which to the idealist are precious if
only partial expressions of spiritual values, are
to him wholly recalcitrant, wholly external and
illusory.   The really precious thing, he says, is
something transcendent, something remote,
something that cannot transpire in events or
body itself in forms, because it is infinite and complete, while these are finite, broken, and limited.
Henri-Frédéric Amiel, a man peculiarly dominated by this way of viewing things, wrote in
his Journal, " Nothing finite is true, is interesting, is worthy to fix my attention.   All that is
particular is exclusive, and all that is exclusive
repels me.   There is nothing non-exclusive but
the All ; my end is communion with Being
through the whole of Being."   Now, whatever
may be the merits of this point of view, it obviously involves a certain degree of artistic failure.   The mystic cannot be entirely successful
in art.   For art depends on organization in
definite forms, and the mystic rejects all particular forms as finite.   " Reality, the present, the
irreparable, the necessary," writes Amiel, " repel

and even terrify me. . . . The life of thought alone seems to me to have enough elasticity and immensity, to be free enough from the irreparable; practical life makes me afraid." Accordingly, men of this temperament are defeated in their search for beauty by an unconquerable shyness of all its incarnations. They fear that in defining their fancy they will vulgarize it. It is their fate to long for an all-inclusive form in a world where forms are mutually exclusive, to strive to utter truth in one great word, when even the shortest sentence must occupy time. Amiel himself is a pathetic example of the mystic's destiny in art. Haunted all his life by the vision of infinite beauty, the conception of absolute truth, he could never bring himself to accept the limitations of all human performance, and his talent was almost as unproductive as it was exalted. He never could embody his aspirations. Tantalizing him with the suggestion of supernal beauties, they resisted all his efforts to come up with and embrace them, because he denied himself the use of those definite forms in which alone, however inadequately, ideals can be realized.

In many respects César Franck is the ana-

logue in music of Amiel in literature. That
vague richness of his emotional tone, which
like a dark background of night is constantly
lighted up by meteoric outbursts of passion, is
strangely like the somber moralizings and spec-
ulations, in the " Journal Intime," among which
Amiel's cries of spiritual pain, doubt, and longing stand out with such sudden, poignant pathos. Franck has in common with Amiel the
mystic's longing for ideal satisfactions, and the
mystic's distrust of all finite means of attaining
them. He, too, is " afraid" of the forms of
practical life, of the conventional devices of musical structure and the types evolved by tradition. He avoids always the obvious, the natural even, and gropes toward some unattainable
ideal of expression. So great is his distrust of
the understood, the accepted, the usual and intelligible, that he is always leaving the beaten
track and roaming afield after some novel and
untamed beauty. It will be worth while to get
to closer quarters with this tendency, and to see
exactly how it operates.

It is hard to make those unacquainted with
musical technique understand how much of
fixity there is in the musical idiom, how defi-

nite are the types of musical form, how potent the requisitions of musical syntax. Yet,
without a sense of this fixity in the material, it
is impossible to estimate justly those impulses
and motives which may lead a composer to vio-
late usages and to disappoint expectations. In
the matter of harmony, for instance, there are
certain types of procedure, certain progressions
and sequences of chords, that are as stable and
uniform as the types of animal or vegetable
form. A horse, a dog, or a man is not a more
definite organism than the two chords in the
" Amen " of a hymn tune. This group or
cluster of two chords, linked together by a
common tone held over from one to the other,
yet made distinct by progression of the other
voices, is typical of a kind of harmonic form
that long usage has established as part of our
mental furniture. We are used to thinking of
chords thus welded by a common tone, and we
demand this sort of coherence in our harmonic
progressions, just as we demand that a horse's
body shall be furnished with a horse's legs, or
that a transitive verb shall have an object. To
be sure, this particular sort of cluster, in which
both chords are, as we say, consonant, is some-

what less determinate than another sort which
we shall describe presently, because, since all the
tones of the first chord are equally important,
any one may be selected as the link, and there
will be consequently some latitude in the choice
of the second chord, which completes the group.
But within these limits this sort of harmonic
type is definite and fixed, and that it is deeply
ingrained in our mode of thought is proved by
our horror of "consecutive octaves" and
"fifths," those bugbears of harmony students,
which are bad chiefly because not compatible
with the retention of a common linking tone
between the two members of the group.

Here we have, then, one of those fundamental harmonic forms which are in music what
idioms or phrases are in language. It is striking how sedulously César Franck, distrustful of
the definite, the conventional, avoids them.
Compared with the work of a keen rationalist
like Saint-Saëns, his music is curiously inco-
herent, curiously loose-knit, groping, and in-
determinate. His pages are studded with de-
partures and evasions; he delights in going
some other way than we expect, or in writing
chords that do not give us even any basis of ex-

pectation. Consecutive octaves and fifths, so terrible to lovers of cogency and sequence, are an especial feature of his harmony, giving it that curious lapsing effect so characteristic and indescribable. His entire tone-mass has a trick of sliding bodily up or down, which disconcerts, even while it fascinates, one who is accustomed to harmonic stability. The student need only play over the opening of the Symphony or the first page of the String Quartet to feel that here is a man who treats traditions debonairly, and who thus suggests novel beauties without defining them.

Equally irresponsible is he in his treatment of another sort of harmonic form which is intrinsically even more definite than the clusters of consonant chords like the " Amen." When there is a dissonant tone in the first chord, a tone which, having slight justification for being, presses urgently toward a neighboring tone in the next chord, into which it is said to "resolve," then the cluster, as a whole, is even more determinate. The dissonance introduces a tension that must be relieved in one definite way. It involves its own resolution just as unstable equilibrium in a body involves its falling in the direction of the greatest pull. The alien tone in the chord is got rid of by the path of least resistance ; it is a foreign element that must be discharged. So potent is this tendency of dissonant tones to resolve that it is one of the chief means of vitalizing the entire musical fabric. Unless music constantly got out of harmony with itself it would no more progress than a man would walk unless before each step he lost his balance. It would stagnate. Consider, for example, the last phrase of that highly vitalized tune, " The Man that Broke the Bank at Monte Carlo." No one could attribute stagnation to this phrase, whatever other faults he might find in it; and its impetus is largely due to the vigor with which it lands on the dissonant chord next before the last, and the consequent pull of this chord into the last. Try to conceive of ending without that last chord, that resolution in which the foreign element is discharged and all comes to rest. It is told of Mendelssohn that he rushed down-stairs in his night clothes early one morning to resolve a dominant seventh chord (such as we have on the syllable " Car ") which some waggish friend struck and left uncompleted. Mendelssohn was of course unusually sensitive to harmonic law, but it is not too much to draw from this incident the conclusion that a chord which can get a man out of bed in the morning to resolve it must pretty potently suggest resolution. Dissonant chords, in fact, are anything but inert elements in the chemistry of harmonic composition. They have strong affinities and combine powerfully.

Yet César Franck is inclined either to ignore these tendencies or to shift them into unexpected and circuitous channels. The dissonant chords, though they occur often in his work, seldom take their normal course. They are led into new dissonances, diverted to alien keys, subjected to ingenious modifications, and in all ways wrested from the realm of the obvious. Towards the end of the Introduction to the first movement of the String Quartet, for instance, the student will find dominant sevenths most interestingly unfaithful to their family tradition, and effecting modulation through distant keys. Similar treatment will be found on almost any page in this Quartet, in the Quintet, the Symphony, and the piano works. Thus, Franck not only goes counter to the less determinate harmonic types in which both chords are consonant, but he loves to disappoint our expectations when they are strongly established by dissonances. Nothing is more characteristic of him than the formal indefiniteness of his harmony. Full as it is of delicious and unwonted beauties, it lacks accurate organization, clarity and solidity of chord sequence. It is a web of shifting tones, without obvious interrelationship and inevitable progression.

When we turn to Franck's treatment of meter and rhythm, we get some new side-lights on the way his mysticism affects his music. He is, in the first place, noticeably lacking in that vigor of pulse, that strong accentuation, which is the delight of active temperaments. He sings constantly, almost never dances. After a while the intensity of the song-like phrases, so packed with emotion, becomes cloying, and we long for a little of the headlong, thoughtless progress of Grieg and Dvořák. We need the relaxation of muscular activity. It would be a relief to stop feeling for a moment and be borne along on a wave of perfectly unemotional " passage-work." But Franck never relieves himself and his hearer by passages of brisk motion in which the interest is entirely active; he is, so to speak, a very sedentary composer. And so the rare beauties that stud the page lose something by being set so thickly. The richness of Franck's emotional impulse is a disadvantage to his metrical structure. The same thing, again, is true of his rhythm or phraseology. We saw in the Introduction how elementary metrical groups—measures—were built up into phrases and tunes, and how the strongest synthetic minds got the greatest variety and breadth of phrase. Now Franck's phrasing, like Grieg's, is of the primitive kind that reveals lack of mental concentration, inability to build up wide and complex forms. Draw a line across his staff at every breathing-point, and your lines will fall pretty regularly after the measures whose numbers are multiples of four. Try the same thing with Beethoven, and there will be no telling where the lines will come, so varied is the phraseology. In comparison, Franck's themes seem hardly more than bundles of motifs, loosely tied together. And of course this effect is unfortunately reinforced by the peculiarities of his harmony. How could a theme hold itself together in such a kaleidoscope?

How could it sustain itself on such a tonal quicksand? Thus his tunes, rich as they are in single phrases of poignant beauty, seldom develop much breadth. They start out well, but soon lose themselves in the web or fall into poorly welded segments. In the larger structural arrangement of his material as well as in his primary metrical order he falls short of the perfect organization of more powerful minds.

Franck illustrates, then, in many ways, in his erratic treatment of harmony, in his metrical monotony, and in his " shortness of breath," the mystic's failure to master form. And yet, so beautiful are his effects, so arresting is his personality, one feels instinctively that there is in him something which destructive criticism cannot assail. The very inarticulateness of the mystic is, in fact, a sort of eloquence, perhaps all the more persuasive because it hints at beauties rather than defines them. However beyond his reach his aspirations may be, so long as they are genuine and ardent he will have his unique artistic message. His work will gain a pathetic appeal from the very fact that it suggests feelings it cannot embody, and his inarticulateness may even open up ways to new modes of utterance by reminding men that there are truths other than those their formulas so smugly stereotype.   Thus a writer like Amiel, ineffective as he seems from one point of view, is not without his liberalizing influence in literature.   In the same way, César Franck, the mystic among musicians, thanks to his profound insight and emotion, combined though they be with the characteristic shortcomings of the seer, will widen the scope of future musical technique and expression.

BIBLIOGRAPHICAL NOTE.—The Prelude, Choral, and Fugue for Piano are to be had in the Collection Litolff. The Prelude, Aria, and Finale are published by J. Hamelle, Paris.   These are the only piano pieces of Franck that are easily obtainable. The house of Hamelle also issues a four-hand arrangement of the Symphony, and Durand, of Paris, publishes a four-hand arrangement of the three masterly Chorals for organ, as well as the original edition of these, and of two sets of organ pieces, one of six and the other of three.   The "Beatitudes" has been reprinted, with English words, by G. Schirmer. A few of Franck's songs, particularly "La Procession," "Panis Angelicus," and "Le Mariage des Roses," will be found in the portfolios of most large music dealers.

VI
PETER ILYITCH
TSCHAÏKOWSKY

PETER ILYITCH TSCHAÏKOWSKY

VI
PETER ILYITCH
TSCHAÏKOWSKY

———

ONE of the constant temptations of the biographer is that of seizing on some salient trait in his subject, magnifying it beyond all relation to others which supplement or modify it, and portraying an eccentric rather than a rounded personality, a monster rather than a man. Human nature is complex, many-sided, even self-contradictory to any but the most penetrative view; and so slender are the resources of literature for dealing with such a paradox as a man, that writers, resorting to simplification, sacrifice fullness to intelligibility. In books Napoleon is apt to be denied all scruples, Keats all virility, Marcus Aurelius all engaging folly; the real men were probably not so simple. It is certain, at any rate, that

Tschaïkowsky, the greatest of Russian musicians, one of the two greatest of all composers
since Wagner, cannot have been the mere incarnation of concentrated gloom that his critics
have drawn.   Some worthier powers than that
of eloquent lamenting must have contributed to
mold him. He was not simply a sort of neurasthenic Jeremiah with a faculty for orchestration.

It is only too easy and plausible, to be sure,
to label him with one of those insidiously
blighting epithets, " neurasthenic," " decadent,"
or " morbid." He was, in fact, of an unfortunate heredity ; his grandfather was epileptic,
and his own symptoms pointed to an inherited
nervous irritability. He was troubled more or
less, all his life, by sleeplessness, fatigue, depression ; and in his thirty-seventh year had a
complete nervous collapse.   But to discredit a
man's insight by pointing out his physical misfortunes is as misleading as it is unkind.   The
fact that Schopenhauer, with whose temperament Tschaïkowsky's had much in common,
had some insane and idiotic ancestors, and suf-
fered much from his own unusual sensitiveness, does not in the least abate the truth of

his philosophic teaching, though it may call attention to its one-sidedness. And so with the musician; knowledge of his personal twist ought not to make us deaf to whatever is universal in his utterance. We may remember that he reports but one aspect of the truth; but if he reports that truly, we may supply the other, and need not carp at the way he got his information. And indeed is it not, after all, an artificial circumscription of life to ignore its sadder verities, however moral Pharisees may stigmatize the perception of them as " morbid "? Has not disease, as well as health, its relation to our fortunes? Is not man's weakness an organic part of his strength, his fear of his courage, his doubt of his faith? That mere facile optimism which smiles blandly at all experience, with unseeing eyes, is as partial and false as the unrelieved pessimism into which the contemplation of it sometimes drives the sensitive. The world is no more all light than it is all shadow. All human life, with its suffering as well as its happiness, is one, and every sincere human experience has its own weight. And so Tschaïkowsky, in spite of grandfathers and symptoms, has a right to be respectfully heard.

The tendency to depreciate men like Tschaï-kowsky and Schopenhauer generally rests on a confusion between what may be called senti-mental and rational pessimism. The sentimental pessimist, the weak malcontent, who sees every-thing through the blue spectacles of egotism, or, like the cuttlefish, muddies his world with a black humor of his own, deserves indeed nothing bet-ter than a shrug.   Like all other forms of senti-mentality, his pessimism is based on selfishness. It is an emanation, not an insight.   It is that form of colic, to use the figure of Thoreau, which makes him discover that the world has been eating green apples.   Quite different from such a sentimentalist, however, is the sensitive man who feels impersonally the real evils of life. Such a man's experience is viewed by him, not as the end, but as the means, of insight. His own pains, however keen, appear to him but as symbols of the universal suf-fering of humanity, and however much his view may be subjectively jaundiced, it does not term-inate in, but only begins with, the petty self. He is not a devotee of the luxury of woe. " A very noble character," says Schopenhauer, " we always conceive with a certain tinge of melan-

choly in it—a melancholy that is anything but
a continual peevishness in view of the daily vex-
ations of life (for such peevishness is an ignoble
trait, and arouses suspicions of maliciousness),
but rather a melancholy that comes from an insight into the vanity of all joys, and the sorrow-
fulness of all living, not alone of one's own fortune." And Tschaïkowsky, in describing
Beethoven's Choral Symphony, writes, one can
see, from precisely the same standpoint : " Such
joy is not of this earth. It is something ideal
and unrealizable ; it has nothing in common
with this life, but is only a momentary aspiration
of humanity towards the holiness which exists
only in the world of art and beauty ; afterwards,
this vale of earth, with its endless sorrow, its
agony of doubt and unsatisfied hopes, seems still
more gloomy and without issue. In the Ninth
Symphony we hear the despairing cry of a great
genius who, having irrevocably lost faith in happiness, escapes for a time into the world of unrealizable hopes, into the realm of broken-
winged ideals." Now undoubtedly these
passages, especially the latter, are guilty of false
emphasis ; undoubtedly one can truly reply to
Tschaïkowsky that the ideal is necessarily fairer

than reality, as the flower is fairer than the soil from which it springs, that " this vale of earth" is not "without issue," however gloomy, since it does in fact produce the ideal world of art and beauty, and that it is precisely the glory of hopes that they are unrealizable, and of happiness that it exists only on a level higher than that of finite life.   But, however one-sided may be the opinions expressed, the attitude of mind is free from the taint of petty selfishness ; it is frank, open-eyed, and manly. Such utterances proceed only from natures nobly human, however burdened with a greater sensibility than is common among men.

Of the extraordinary sensibility of Tschaï-kowsky, his emotional intensity and impetuosity, which, discerning truly, critics have so often falsely interpreted, there can be no doubt. He was the subject and in some ways the victim, of hereditary instability, a tendency, so to speak, to go off at half-cock. In his life no trait comes out more conspicuously, and its association with his powerful intellect, with which it was always at odds, goes far to explain the anomalies and paradoxes of his music. We see it constantly in his acts, where, if we always remember that we are studying a great nature, which must be analyzed respectfully and without vulgar curiosity, we may learn much from observing it.

Peter Ilyitch Tschaïkowsky was born in a small Russian town in 1840. As a very small boy he showed his ardent patriotism by kissing the map of Russia, in his Atlas, and spitting at the rest of Europe. When his French nurse remonstrated, he explained that he had been careful to cover France with his hand. There already is his temperament—passionate and tender. The Tschaïkowsky family early moved to St. Petersburg, where Peter at first entered the School of Jurisprudence, and later obtained a post in the Ministry of Justice. All through his youth he was indolent, popular, fond of society, a graceful amateur who played *salon* pieces at evening parties. That his serious interest in music was first aroused by his cousin's showing him how to "modulate" is rather amusing when we remember the virtuosity and daring of his mature harmonic style. "My cousin said it was possible to modulate from one key to another," he says, "without using more than three chords. This excited my curiosity, and to my astonishment I found that he improvised whatever modulations I suggested, even from quite extraneous keys." In 1861 he wrote to his sister that he was meditating a musical career, but was still in doubt whether he could pursue it successfully. "Perhaps idleness may take possession of me, and I may not persevere." But a little later all doubts had vanished, he had given up his official work, withdrawn from society, and thrown himself with characteristic ardor into his studies. He now sometimes sat up all night working, and Rubinstein, his composition teacher at the Conservatory, tells how on one occasion he submitted no less than two hundred variations on a single theme. He made such good progress that in 1866, a few years after his graduation, he was appointed professor of harmony in the Moscow Conservatory.

From about this time date his first important compositions. "When first he came to live in Moscow," writes his friend M. Kashkin, "although he was then six-and-twenty, he was still inexperienced and young in many things, especially in the material questions of life; but in all that concerned his work he was already mature, with a particularly elaborate method of work, in which all was foreseen with admirable judgment, and manipulated with the exactitude of the surgeon in operating." M. Kashkin's testimony is a valuable corrective to the widespread impression that Tschaïkowsky composed in a mad frenzy of passion. No good work, in art any more than in science, is done without that calm deliberation which his strong mental grasp made possible to him. His early compositions were for the most part operas, and, it must be added, unsuccessful operas. " The Voievoda," written in 1866, did not satisfy him, and he burned the score. " Undine," composed in 1870, was not accepted by the theatrical authorities, who moreover mislaid the manuscript; Tschaïkowsky, years later, recovered and destroyed it. In 1873 " Snegourotchka," a ballet, in spite of some musical beauty, failed for lack of dramatic interest. The success of " Kouznetz Vakoula," produced a year later, was ephemeral. Thus it was not until " The Oprichnik," which still holds the stage in Russia, was brought out, when Tschaïkowsky was thirty-four, that he made a pronounced success. The persistence with which he continued to labor during these years seems to be overlooked by those who consider him a mere prophet of lassitude and discouragement. Nor would such a man have undertaken and discharged the drudgery of journalistic criticism as did Tschaïkowsky in the four years from 1872 to 1876, when he was writing critiques for the Moscow papers. Whatever fluctuations of mood he may have undergone in these early years, and we may be sure they were many, his outward life was an example of equability, diligence and patience.

In 1877, however, there was some sort of tragic happening. That it was somehow connected with an unhappy marriage, that it resulted in a complete nervous breakdown, these things we know.* It is unnecessary to probe for more specific details; it is enough to note that for a long time he was broken and despairing, that through all the rest of his life his

---

* Since the present paper was written, the biography of Tschaïkowsky by his brother has shown that in this unhappy marriage the only fault we can attribute to the composer was a quixotic chivalry in marrying a young woman who had declared her love for him. He married her from sympathy without loving her. Of course such a step could lead to nothing but misery; but however unwise, it was at least generous and honorable.

mental temper, never bright, was shadowed with a pathological gloom. He left the Conservatory suddenly, and was abroad a year. He wrote one of his friends, "On the whole, I am robust; but as regards my soul, there is a wound there that will never heal. I think I am *homme fini*. . . . Something is broken in me; my wings are cut and I shall never fly very high again." He says that had he remained a day longer in Moscow he should have drowned himself, and it is said that he did go so far, in his terrible depression, as to stand up to his chest in the river one frosty September night, "in the hope of literally catching his death of cold, and getting rid of his troubles without scandal."

But he took the better way; indeed, the best years, the quietest and most fruitful years, of his life were yet before him. As robust in character as he was sensitive and impetuous in temperament, he pulled himself together, and wrote in the next year his masterly Fourth Symphony, his best opera, "Eugene Oniegin," said to be the second most popular opera in Russia, and many other strong works. He returned also, in the fall of 1878, to his post at the Conservatory, but, by the generosity of an anonymous lady,* was soon enabled to give up teaching and devote himself entirely to composition. From this time on, except for a conducting tour through western Europe in 1888, and one to America a few years later, he stayed chiefly in the country, in studious solitude. His mode of life at Maidanova, a little village where in 1885 he took a house, has been described by M. Kashkin, who often visited him. After working all the morning, and taking a simple but well-cooked dinner, Tschaïkowsky always went for a long walk, no matter what the weather. "Many of his works were planned and his themes invented," we are told, "in these long rambles across country." After tea he worked again until supper-time, and after supper the two friends, ordering a bottle of wine and dismissing the servant, would devote themselves to playing four-hand music. M. Kashkin tells one or two interesting stories of Tschaïkowsky at this period. His impulsiveness, it seems,

---

* This lady, according to the new biography, was Frau von Meck, the widow of a wealthy railway engineer. Her interest in Tschaikowsky's work, and her generous gifts of money, were of great value to him all his life.

took the form in money matters of a fairly reckless generosity. So lavishly did he shower coppers on all the peasant children in the neighborhood, that he could not go for his walk without being surrounded by them. In one afternoon he is said to have dispensed fourteen shillings of his own and all of M. Kashkin's small change. A friend once asked him where he "invested his capital." Convulsed with laughter, he answered that his last investment of capital had been in a Moscow hotel, and that where his next would be he did not know.

The events of his tour in 1888 he has himself narrated with characteristic modesty and charm, in a fragment of diary. One can read between the lines that he was everywhere the center of admiring interest, but with fine literary instinct he constantly subordinates himself to the people and events through which he moved. How lovable are his vainly continued efforts to enjoy the music of Brahms, his eagerness to record the little kindnesses of his friends, his dignified reticence about his enemies, his hearty appreciation of work far inferior to his own! "I trust," he says, "that it will not appear like self-glorification that my dithyramb in praise of Grieg precedes the statement that our natures are closely allied. Speaking of Grieg's high qualities, I do not at all wish to impress my readers with the notion that I am endowed with an equal share of them. I leave it to others to decide how far I am lacking in all that Grieg possesses in such abundance." This warm appreciation of others, combined with so pathetic a lack of self-confidence that on more than one occasion he burned the score of a work which was coldly received, was so extreme in Tschaïkowsky that one of his friends pronounced him the least conceited of composers. Like all sensitive people, indeed, he was painfully conscious of social bonds ; what was due him from others, and what in turn was due them from him —these intangibles, so easily forgotten by most men, were to him heavy realities. It is touching to see how dependent he was on the friendliness of the orchestra he was leading, and he was so impressible by criticism that long after his fame was established he could repeat word for word Hanslick's and Cui s early attacks upon him. On the other hand, M. Kashkin says that when he was conducting the works of others he was so sensible of his responsibility that his face wore a look of physical pain. When he was dying of cholera, in terrible agony, he thanked all about his bedside for the consideration they showed him, and his last remark reminds one of Charles the Second's "I am afraid, gentlemen, I am an unconscionable time a-dying." He turned to his nephews after an unusually severe attack of nausea with the exclamation, "What a state I am in! You will have but little respect for your uncle when you think of him in such a state as this!" He died at St. Petersburg, in October, 1893.

By this time it will be clear enough that this was no puling complainer, but a delicate, high nature of great emotional intensity, subjected to a cruel interaction of temperament and circumstances, and yet capable of nobly constructive artistic work. His life, candidly examined, reveals modesty, dignity, elevation of ideal and of character. Yet it does illustrate, too, in many ways, that lack of emotional balance which underlies the peculiar quality of his music.

His mere method of approaching his art, in the first place, is significant. All his early efforts, as we have seen, were operas; he wrote altogether ten operas, and the Pathetic Symphony is the last fruit of a genius dramatic rather than symphonic. At thirty Tschaïkowsky was unable to read orchestral scores with ease, and preferred to study the classics through four-hand arrangements, while his distaste for the purest form of music was so great that he protested he could hardly keep awake through the performance of the masterly A-minor Quartet of Beethoven. This attitude toward the string quartet, which is in music what engraving or etching is in representative art, is very anomalous in a young composer, and shows so disproportionate an interest in the merely expressive side of music that it is hard to understand how Tschaïkowsky ever became so great a plastic master as his last two symphonies, for all their freight of passion, show him to be.

He never, in fact, wholly outgrew certain peculiarities which are direct results of his emotional instability, his slavery to mood. His persistent use of minor keys, for example, is, as the doctors say, symptomatic. The minor is naturally the medium of vague, subjective moods and fantasies, of aspiration, longing, and doubt; it is the vehicle of morbidly self-bounded thoughts, whose depressing gloom is equalled only by their seductive and malign beauty. Such thoughts we find too often in Chopin, Grieg, and, it must be added, in Tschaïkowsky. Of the first thirty songs he wrote, seventeen are in the minor mode. Of course too much should not be argued from a detail of this sort, but the major system is so naturally the medium of vigorously objective thought that we instinctively suspect the health of a mind which harps continually upon the minor. By a somewhat similar tendency towards self-involution, the natural result of intense emotionality, Tschaïkowsky inclines to monotony of rhythm; he gets hypnotized, as it were, by the regular pulsation of some recurring meter, and he continues it to the verge of trance. An example is the long pedal-point on D, in the curious 5-4 measure of the second movement of the Pathetic Symphony. This is like the wailing and rocking of the women of a savage tribe over the death of a warrior; it is at once wild and sinister. But perhaps the most striking evidence of this servitude to passion we are trying to trace in Tschaïkowsky is his constant use of climax. It seems to be quite impossible for him to preserve a mean-tone; he is always lashing himself into a fury, boiling up into a frenetic fortissimo, after which he lapses into coma until some phrase of melody or impulse of rhythm jostles his imagination again, and he presses on toward a new crisis. The effect of these cumulative whirlwinds of passion is often tremendous, is unique, indeed, in music; yet one longs sometimes in the midst of them for a less turbulent attitude, for the equable beauty of Bach or Mozart. The atmosphere is surcharged. One feels that this noble but willful spirit has sat too long in the close chamber of personal feeling, that one must throw wide the windows and let in the fresh winds of general human existence.

Yet, after all, the imperfections of Tschaïkowsky's music are due rather to the overwhelming richness of his emotions than to any shortcomings of mind; his case is an artistic embarrassment of riches, and his critic must avoid the fallacy of supposing, because his constructive power is sometimes inadequate, that it is ever meager. On the contrary, he is a man of great intellectual force. It is too bad to be so busy with Tschaïkowsky the pessimist that one forgets Tschaïkowsky the artist His melodic fertility alone is enough to rank him with the great constructive musicians. His devotion to Mozart, and to the Italian opera-writers, was no accident ; by the spontaneity and beauty of his melodies he has " approved himself their worthy brother." Few more inspiring tunes can be found anywhere than the opening theme of his B-flat minor Piano Concerto, with its splendid and tireless vigor, or the broad, constantly unfolding cantilena of the second theme in the Fifth Symphony. His pages are plentifully scattered with phrases of rare grace, of a fresh and original charm. His harmony, too, for all its radicalism, is generally firm and well controlled, and his rhythm, however monotonous at times, is never vague. In polyphony (the simultaneous progress of different melodies) he is a powerful master, as any one may see by examining, for example, the masterly variations in his Orchestral Suite, opus 55. He is probably, on the whole, a greater master of general construction than any of his contemporaries except Brahms.

It is evident, then, that this curiously para-

doxical personality was gifted with an intellectual strength that went far toward dominating
the turbulent passions which, on the whole, it
could not quite dominate.   But one needs, after
all, no careful statistical proof of the rationality
of Tschaïkowsky's music.   The fact that it
survives, that it is widely listened to and loved,
proves *a priori* that, however tinged it may be
with personal melancholy, it is not ultimately
pessimistical or destructive in effect.   For it is
the happy fortune of art that it cannot fully
voice the destructive forces of anarchy and despair.   Its nature precludes the possibility, for
anarchy is chaos, despair is confusion, and neither
can be the subject of that clearly organic order
which is art.   The artist may, of course, express
sadness ; his work, if it is to be comprehensively
human, must be reflective of the ebb as well as
the flow of vital power.   But it cannot mirror
complete dejection, the absolute lapse of power ;
for without power there is no organization, and
without organization there is no art.   The melodic invention, the harmonic grasp, the rhythmic vigor, in a word the powerful musical articulation, everywhere present in Tschaïkowsky's
best work, remove it far from the inarticulate

moanings of despair. Such faculties as his are anything but disintegrating or decadent; however much individual sadness may attend their exercise, they are upbuilding and creative. Tschaïkowsky commands our admiration more than our pity because, in spite of the burdens of his temperament and the misfortunes of his experience, he contributed to beauty, and beauty is the standing confutation of evil.

BIBLIOGRAPHICAL NOTE.—Much of Tschaikowsky's early work was for piano, but most of his piano pieces are light if not trivial in character. They are amusing to play over, but do not fairly represent his genius. Seventeen of them are to be had in an album in the Collection Litolff. The Sonata, op. 37, on the other hand, in spite of its marked resemblance to Schumann's F-sharp minor Sonata, is one of the finest of modern sonatas for piano. The Concertos are masterly, but very difficult. Most of the important orchestral works are arranged for four hands. The most interesting are the Pathetic Symphony, the Fifth Symphony, which should be equally well known, the Orchestral Suites, particularly the third, op. 55, with its charming *Tema con Variazioni*, and the Overture, Romeo and Juliet. Of the chamber-works, the third String Quartet, op. 30, and the Trio, are especially good. Twenty-four of Tschaikowsky's songs are published in an album by Novello, Ewer & Co., and many separately by G. Schirmer and others.

VII
JOHANNES BRAHMS

JOHANNES BRAHMS

JOHANNES BRAHMS

—

O F all the figures of modern music, brilliant and varied as they are, impressing one with the many-sidedness and wide scope of the art, there is perhaps only one, that of Johannes Brahms, which conveys the sense of satisfying poise, self-control and sanity. Others excel him in particular qualities. Grieg is more delicate and intimate, Dvořák warmer and clearer in color; Saint-Saëns is more meteoric, Franck more recondite and subtle, and Tschaïkowsky more impassioned; but Brahms alone has Homeric simplicity, the primeval health of the well-balanced man. He excels all his contemporaries in soundness and universality. In an age when many people are uncertain of themselves and the world, victims of a pervasive unrest and disap-

pointment, it is solacing to find so heroic and
simple a soul, who finds life acceptable, meets
it genially, and utters his joy and his sorrow
with the old classic sincerity. He is not blighted
by any of the myriad forms of egotism,—by
sentimentality, by the itch to be effective at all
costs, or to be "original," or to be Byronic or
romantic or unfathomable. He has no "message" for an errant world; no anathema, either
profoundly gloomy or insolently clever, to hurl
at God. He has rather a deep and broad impersonal love of life; universal joy is the sum and
substance of his expression.

It is hard to say whether the unique greatness of Brahms depends more on this emotional wholesomeness and simplicity or on the
intellectual breadth and synthetic power with
which it is combined. Probably the truth is
that true greatness requires the interaction
of the two. At any rate, Brahms is equally remarkable, whether considered as a man or as a
musician, for both. In his personal character
frankness, modesty, simple and homely virtue
were combined with the widest sympathy, the
most far-ranging intelligence, extreme catholicity and tolerance. In music he prized equally

the simplest elements, like the old German folk-songs and the Hungarian dances, and the most complex artistic forms that are evolved from them by creative genius. Like Bach and Beethoven, he spanned the whole range of human interests; deep feeling fills his music with primitive expressiveness, and at the same time great intellectual power gives it the utmost scope and complexity. Lacking either trait he would not have been himself, he could not have performed his service to music.

There are many anecdotes illustrating the simple, large traits of the man. His pleasures were homely, his ambitions inward and vital. He cared little for fame, and was annoyed by the foolish adulation of the crowd. To a long and flowery speech addressed to him on the presentation of some sort of tribute he answered, with admirable brevity and utter prose, "Thank you very much." Once when a party of his friends were gathered together to sample a rare old wine, somebody pompously announced, "What Brahms is among the composers, this Rauenthaler is among the wines." "Ah," snapped out Brahms, "then let's have a bottle of Bach now." He often remarked that one could never hope to get upon the level of such giants as Bach and Beethoven; one could only work conscientiously in one's own field. He had the disgust of shams that one expects in so sincere a lover of the genuine, and the armor of roughness and sarcasm with which he protected himself against the pretentious was formidable. When the University of Cambridge offered him a degree, suggesting that he write a new work for the occasion, he replied that if any of his old works seemed good enough to them he should be happy to receive the honor, but that he was too busy to write a new one. There was about him something shaggy, bearlike, and one can imagine the foxes and weasels scattering at his growl.

But for everything fresh and genuine Brahms had the heartiest love. He is one of the innumerable army of great men of whom biography loves to relate that they always carried candy in their pockets for the children, and a lady described in a letter how she had seen him on the hotel piazza, on all-fours, clambered over by young playmates. He was on cordial terms with waiters and servants, and told Mr. Henschel with emotion the story of a serving-maid who lost her position in order to shield a careless postman, who, being married, could not afford to lose his. Another pretty story, showing at once his modesty and his catholicity of taste, recounts how all the musical friends of the wife of Johann Strauss, the great waltz composer, were writing their names, with phrases from their works, on her fan. When it was his turn, the composer of the German Requiem wrote the opening phrase of the " Blue Danube" waltz, and underneath it the words, " Not, I regret to say, by your devoted friend, Johannes Brahms." Thus wholesome and unaffected was the character of this great man.

Outwardly, Brahms's life was uneventful. His father was a contrabass-player in the theatre orchestra of Hamburg. In him his son's positiveness of character seems to have been foreshadowed, for we learn that when the conductor once directed him not to play so loud, he replied with dignity : " Herr Capellmeister, this is my contrabass, I want you to understand, and I shall play on it as loud as I please." Brahms was born at Hamburg in 1833, and from his earliest years was trained for music as a matter of course. His early acquaintance with the

best works was of incalculable value to him.
Mr. Hadow points out that the eclecticism and
solidity of his style was doubtless largely due to
the study of Bach and Beethoven that he made
in youth under Marxsen. He had the advantage, too, of early practical experience. When
he was only twenty he made a concert tour with
Reményi, the Hungarian violinist, during which
he gained much training and confidence. A
feat he performed during this trip showed even
more virtuosity than that of " le petit Saint-
Saëns " already recorded. Having to play the
Kreutzer Sonata on a piano too low in pitch
to suit Reményi, who disliked to tune down his
violin, he transposed it up a semi-tone, and
though playing without notes, performed it accurately and with spirit. To this feat, which
aroused the admiration of Joachim, Brahms
owed his acquaintance with the great violinist,
and through him with Liszt and Schumann.
His experience with the former, then in the
height of his fame, was unfortunate, but characteristic. Brahms, who was worn out with travel,
fell asleep during one of the most moving parts
of Liszt's Sonata, which the great virtuoso was
so condescending as to play.   Though Brahms

was only a boy at the time, he was evidently, even then, undazzled by worldly glory.

His meeting with Schumann was much more happy; indeed, it was one of the important events of his life. Probably no young composer ever received such a hearty welcome into the musical world as Schumann extended to Brahms in his famous article, "New Paths." "In sure and unfaltering accents," writes Mr. Hadow, "he proclaimed the advent of a genius in whom the spirit of the age should find its consummation and its fulfilment; a master by whose teaching the broken phrases should grow articulate, and the vague aspirations gather into form and substance. The five-and-twenty years of wandering were over; at last a leader had arisen who should direct the art into 'new paths,' and carry it a stage nearer to its appointed place." It is not surprising that Schumann, whose generous enthusiasm often led him to praise worthless work, should have received the early compositions of Brahms so cordially. Their qualities were such as to affect profoundly the great romanticist. Although the essential character of his mature works is their classical balance and restraint, these first compositions show an exuberance, a wayward fertility of invention, thoroughly romantic. His first ten opuses, or at any rate the three sonatas and the four ballades for piano, are frequently turgid in emotion, and ill-considered in form. The massive vigor of his later work here appears in the guise of a cyclopean violence. It is small wonder that Schumann, dazzled, delighted, overwhelmed, gave his ardent support to the young man. Brahms now found himself suddenly famous. He was discussed everywhere, his pieces were readily accepted by publishers, and his new compositions were awaited with interest.

But fortunate as all this was for Brahms, it might easily, but for his own good sense and self-control, have turned out the most unfortunate thing that could happen to him. For consider his position. He was a brilliant young composer who had been publicly proclaimed by one of the highest musical authorities. He was expected to go on producing works; he was almost under obligation to justify his impressive introduction. Not to do so would be much worse than to remain a nonentity; it would be to become one. And he had meanwhile every internal reason for meeting people's demands.

He was full of ideas, conscious of power, under inward as well as outward compulsion to express himself. Yet for all that, he was in reality immature, unformed, and callow. His work, for all its brilliancy, was whimsical and subjective. If he had followed out the path he was on, as any contemporary observer would have expected, he would have become one of the most radical of romanticists. At thirty he would have been a bright star in the musical firmament, at forty he would have been one of several bright stars, at fifty he would have been clever and disappointed. It required rare insight in so young a man, suddenly successful, to realize the danger, rare courage to avert it. When we consider the temptation it must have been to him to continue these easy triumphs, when we imagine the inward enthusiasm of creation with which he must have been on fire, we are ready to appreciate the next event of the drama.

That event was withdrawal from the musical world and the initiation of a long course of the severest study. When he was a little over twenty-one, Brahms imposed upon himself this arduous training, and commanded himself to forego for a while the eloquent but ill-controlled expression hitherto his, in order to acquire a broader, firmer, purer, and stronger style. For four or five years, to borrow Stevenson's expression, he "played the sedulous ape" to Bach and Beethoven, and in a minor degree to Haydn and Mozart. The complex harmonies of his first period gave place to simple, strong successions of triads; for an emotional and often vague type of melody he substituted clearly crystallized, fluent, and gracious phrases, frequently devoid of any particular expression; the whimsical rhythms of the piano sonatas were followed by the square-cut sections of the Serenade, opus 11. Of course the immediate effect of all this was a great sacrifice of what is called originality; had Brahms not had complete faith in the vitality of his genius he could not have surrendered so much of immediate attainment for the sake of an ultimately greater mastery. It is a profound lesson in the ethics of art that a man who could write the fourth of the Ballades, opus 10, should have been willing to follow it up with this Serenade, opus 11. Yet Brahms knew what he was about, and his first large work, the Piano Concerto, opus 15, shows his individuality of expression entirely regained, and now with immensely increased power and resource.

Nothing could exhibit better than this dissatisfaction with his early work and withdrawal from the world for study, that intellectual breadth which we have noted as characteristic of Brahms. He was not a man who could be content with a narrow personal expression. No subjective heaven could satisfy him. His wide human sympathy and his passion for artistic perfection alike, compelled him to study unremittingly, to widen his ideals as his powers increased. No fate could seem to him so horrible as that " setting " of the mind which is the æsthetic analogue of selfishness. Originality, which so often degenerates into idiosyncrasy, was much less an object to him than universality, which is after all the best means of being serviceably original. Dr. Deiters, in his reminiscences, after describing this period of study, continues: " Henceforth we find him striving after moderation, endeavoring to place himself more in touch with the public, and to conquer all subjectiveness. To arrive at perspicuity and precision of invention, clear design and form, careful elaboration and accurate balancing of effect, now became with him essential and established principles."

From this time until the end of his life, in fact, a period of only a little less than forty years—he died in 1897—Brahms never departed from the modes of work and the ideals of attainment he had now set himself. He labored indefatigably, but with no haste or impatience. He was too painstaking and conscientious a workman to botch his products by hurrying them. He thus described to his friend, Mr. Henschel, his method of composing: "There is no real *creating* without hard work. That which you would call invention, that is to say, a thought, is simply an inspiration from above, for which I am not responsible, which is no merit of mine. Yes, it is a present, a gift, which I ought even to despise until I have made it my own by right of hard work. And there need be no hurry about that either. It is as with the seed corn : it germinates unconsciously and in spite of ourselves. When I, for instance, have found the first phrase of a song, I might shut the book there and then, go for a walk, do some other work, and perhaps not think of it again for months. Nothing, however, is lost.

If afterward I approach the subject again, it is sure to have taken shape ; I can now really begin to work at it." Another inkling of the severity of his standard we have in a remark he made after pointing out certain imperfections in a song of Mr. Henschel's. "Whether it is beautiful also," he said, "is an entirely different matter ; but perfect it must be." With such a standard, we need not be surprised that he imposed so severe a training upon himself at twenty-one, or that he continued all his life the practice of writing each day a contrapuntal exercise, or that he wrought for ten years over his first symphony, that Titanic work. Thus laboring always with the same calm persistence, returning upon his ideas until he could present them with perfect clarity, caring little for the indifference or the applause of the public, but much for the approval of his own fastidious taste, he produced year by year an astonishing series of masterpieces. No one has better described the kind of work that made Brahms great than Matthew Arnold in those lines about labor

> " which in lasting fruit outgrows
> Far noisier schemes ; accomplished in repose ;
> Too great for haste, too high for rivalry."

A just conception of this broad scheme of Brahms's ideal and of his thoroughness in working it out is necessary, we must insist, not only to appreciation of the man himself, but to any true understanding of his relation and service to music. Brahms was enabled, by the tireless training to which he subjected his fertile and many-sided genius, to couch romantic feeling in classic form. In order to grasp the full significance of such a work, it is necessary to bear in mind those fundamental principles of musical effect and facts of musical history which have been presented in the Introduction. Music has resulted from the gradual formal definition, by time and pitch relations, of those vague gestures and utterances by which men expressed their primitive feelings. It has been, in a word, the product of two human instincts, neither of which alone would have sufficed to produce it —the instinct for expression and the instinct for beauty. But these instincts have not worked with precisely equal efficacy at all times. In fact, so limited is human attention, so few things can men attend to at once, every great development of expression has generally disturbed the equilibrium requisite to beauty, and every great advance in beauty has generally, for the time being, restrained the eloquence of expression. Musical history is a series of reactions between man's primal emotional impulse and his desire for intelligibility. First, urgency of feeling drives him to a formless cry; then the wish to be understood and the love of beauty induce him to formulate this cry; finally, as soon as the formula is felt to be inadequate to further expression, it is discarded in favor of one more elastic and complex. The conventions that are helpful at one stage prove hindrances in the next. The same forms that subserve growth up to a certain point, beyond that point hamper it. Accordingly, in the history of music, formulation has always been followed by relaxation of the formulæ to admit of new expression; and when new expression has been thus evolved, a new and more complex form has had to be worked out to regulate and fix it.

Such a period of relaxation was that which intervened between Beethoven and Brahms. The romanticists, headed by Schumann, seized upon the possibilities of poignant expression that they were quick to recognize in their

heritage from Beethoven, and developed an extraordinarily mobile and eloquent instrument for
voicing personal emotion.   At the same time
they inevitably lost the perfect control of form,
the transparent lucidity of structure, that had
characterized Beethoven.   In some respects
more moving, they were on the whole less intelligible.   They were enriching their art, and
must leave the perfect subordination of the new
material to their successors.   It is most interesting to trace the analogy between this development of musical expression and the growth
of emotional life in the individual, and to observe how in both the period of experience, in
which emotion is felt in all its immediate stress,
inhibiting all else and being therefore conceived
in no relations, but merely as a single and ultimate fact, is followed by the period of medita-
tion and self-inspection, when the whole emotional life is grouped into order, and the man
learns to see the significance and the spiritual
value of his feelings. With the romanticists music
necessarily became more and more the medium
of personal passion, less and less the revealer
of universal order.

Browning, himself a romanticist through and

through, has summed up the spirit of romanticism in a single stanza of his " Old Pictures
in Florence " :

> " On which I conclude, that the early painters,
> To cries of 'Greek art and what more wish you ? '
> Replied, ' To become now self-acquainters,
> And paint man, man, whatever the issue !
> Make new hopes shine through the flesh they fray,
> New fears aggrandize the rags and tatters :
> To bring the invisible full into play !
> Let the visible go to the dogs—what matters ?' "

The individualism, the subjectivity, the mystical distrust of definite forms, so stirringly cham-
pioned in these lines, are vital principles in the
work of all the composers of the generation after
Beethoven. Thus in Schumann's music, for
example, the generality of the emotional burden
of classical music is changed to something far
more individual and introspective. Expression
is more tinged by temperament ; the work of art
exhales a personal fragrance. Schumann tells
us not merely of love, longing, and passion, but
of Robert Schumann's love, longing, and passion. His work, for all its beauty, is much less
inclusive and complete than the classical masterpieces. In the same way Chopin filled his noc-

turnes and preludes with the lovely but often
unhealthy poetry of the isolated dreamer, and
Wagner, separating the passion of love from the
other interests of the heart, and thus throwing
out of balance the spiritual economy, sacrificed
as much in health as he gained in potency.
And of the men we have been studying, Grieg,
Franck, and Tschaïkowsky also illustrate in various ways the tendency to " paint man, man,
whatever the issue," to let the " flesh be frayed "
and the " visible go to the dogs." It is hardly
necessary to say that all these men have their
legitimate place. Their message of passion and
unrest, already audible in Beethoven, was the
inevitable and indispensable expression of one
of those self-conscious phases in man's growth
when he freshly realizes his finitude. Their utterances make a deeply pathetic appeal to us,
because they reveal all the terrible sadness of
personal life which as yet finds no resting-place
in the universal. Aspiration and disappointment, bitter grief and blind pain, speak in their
fragmentary loveliness. The romanticists will
never want for our love, since they interpret to
us a part of our own experience.

But, as we have said, after man suffers emotion he reflects upon it; after he feels the parts he learns the whole; after musicians have developed new capabilities of expression they proceed to subordinate them to plastic beauty. Adjustment follows discovery, and the romantic takes on classical perfection. The chaos of one age is thus the order of the next; and after Schumann and his fellows had enriched the world with their beautiful but fragmentary and wayward feelings, it remained for Brahms to essay a further conquest; to commence at least (and perhaps he has not done more) the task of making these new feelings more intelligible, of clarifying their turgidity, of subordinating their conflicts in a more complex harmony. Or, to state his function in more specifically musical terms, he had to discover how rugged melodic outlines, bold harmonic progressions, and the large-spanned phrases of modern musical thought could be organized and brought into that unity in variety which is beauty.

We are now in a position to grasp the full significance of that severe training to which Brahms subjected himself in his youth. Without it he would have gone on doing brilliant work of the romantic order, like his first compositions, but he would never have attained the grasp and self-control that raised him above all his contemporaries and that made possible his peculiar service to music. That period of training was the artistic counterpart of what many men undergo when they discover how many sacrifices and how long a labor are necessary to him who would find a spiritual dwelling-place on earth. Many pleasures must be renounced before happiness will abide; evil and suffering are opaque save to the steadfast eye. So, in music, effects and eloquences and crises must be the handmaids of orderly beauty, and tones are stubborn material until one has learned by hard work to make them transmit thoughts. Technic is in the musician what character is in the man. It is the power to stamp matter with spirit. Brahms's long apprenticeship was therefore needed in the first place to make him master of his materials; in the second place to teach him the deeper lesson that the part must be subordinated to the whole, or, in musical language, expression to beauty.

He achieved this subordination, however, not by the negative process of suppression, but by conquest and co-ordination. In his music

emotion is not excluded, it is regulated; his
work is not a reversion to an earlier and simpler
type, it is the gathering and fusing together of
fragmentary new elements, resulting in a more
complex organism. Thus it is a very superficial view to say that he "went back" to
Beethoven. He drew guidance from the same
natural laws that had guided Beethoven, but he
applied these laws to a material of novel thought
and emotion that had come into being after
Beethoven. Had he repudiated the new material, even for the reason that he considered it
incapable of organization, he would have been
a pedant, which is to say a musical Pharisee.
One masters by recognizing and using, not by
repudiating. And just as a wise man will not
become ascetical merely because his passions
give him trouble, but will study to find out
their true relation to *him* and then keep them
in it, so Brahms recognized the wayward beauties of romanticism, and studied how to make
them ancillary to that order and fair proportion
which is the soul of music.

To this great artistic service he was fitted by
both the qualities which have been pointed out
above as coöperating to form his unique nature.

His deep and simple human feeling, which put him in sympathy with the aims of the romanticists and enabled him to grasp their meaning, would not have sufficed alone; but fortunately it was associated with an almost unprecedented scope of intellect and power of synthesis. Brahms's assimilative faculty was enormous. Like a fine tree that draws the materials of its beauty through a thousand roots that reach into distant pockets of earth, he gathered the materials of his perfectly unified and transparent style from all sorts of forgotten nooks and crannies of mediæval music. Spitta remarks his use of the old Dorian and Phrygian modes; of complex rhythms that had long fallen into disuse; of those means of thematic development, such as augmentation and diminution, which flourished in the fifteenth and sixteenth centuries; of "the *basso ostinato* with the styles pertaining to it—the Passacaglia and the Ciaconna;" and of the old style of variations, in which the bass rather than the melody is the feature retained. "No musician," Spitta concludes, "was more well read in his art or more constantly disposed to appropriate all that was new, especially all newly discovered treasures of the past. His passion for learning wandered, indeed, into every field, and resulted in a rich and most original culture of mind, for his knowledge was not mere acquirement, but became a living and fruitful thing."

The vitality of his relation with the past is nowhere more strikingly shown than in his indebtedness to the two greatest masters of pure music, Bach and Beethoven. He has gathered up the threads of their dissimilar styles, and knitted them into one solid fabric. The great glory of Bach, as is well-known, was his wonderful polyphony. In his work every voice is a melody, everything sings, there is no dead wood, no flaccid filling. Beethoven, on the other hand, turning to new problems, to problems of structure which demanded a new sort of control of key-relationship and the thematic development of single "subjects" or tunes, necessarily paid less attention to the subordinate voices. His style is homophonic or one-voiced rather than polyphonic. The interest centres in one melody and its evolutions, while the others fall into the subordinate position of accompaniment. But Brahms, retaining and extending the complexity of structure, the architectural variety and solidity, that was Beethoven's great achievement, has succeeded in giving new melodic life also to the inner parts, so that the significance and interest of the whole web remind one of Bach. His skill as a contrapuntist is as notable as his command of structure. Thanks to his wonderful power of assimilating methods, of adapting them to the needs of his own expression, so that he remains personal and genuine while becoming universal in scope, he is the true heir and comrade of Bach and Beethoven.

It was, perhaps, inevitable that in his great work of synthesis and formulation he should sometimes be led into dry formalism. One who concerns himself so indefatigably with the technic of construction naturally comes to take a keen joy in the exercise of his skill; and this may easily result, when thought halts, in the fabrication of ingenuities and Chinese puzzles. Some pages of Brahms consist of infinitely dexterous manipulations of meaningless phrases. And though one must guard against assuming that he is dry whenever one does not readily follow him, it certainly must be confessed that sometimes he seems to write merely for the sake of writing. This occasional over-intellectualism, morever, is unfortunately aggravated by a lack of feeling for the purely sensuous side of music, for clear, rich tone-combination, to which Brahms must plead guilty. His orchestra is often muddy and hoarse, his piano style often shows neglect of the necessities of sonority and clearness. Dr. William Mason testifies that his touch was hard and unsympathetic, and it is rather significant of insensibility or indifference to tone color that his Piano Quintet was at first written for strings alone, and that the Variations on a Theme of Haydn exist in two forms, one for orchestra and the other for two pianos, neither of which is announced as the original version. There is danger of exaggerating the importance of such facts, however. Austere and somber as Brahms's scoring generally is, itmay be held that so it should be to be in keeping with the musical conception. And if his piano style is novel it is not really unidiomatic or without its own peculiar effects.

However extreme we may consider the weakness of sensuous perception, which on the whole cannot be denied in Brahms, it is the only serious flaw in a man equally great on the emo-

tional and the intellectual sides.   Very remarkable is the richness and at the same time the
balance of Brahms's nature.   He recognized
early in life that feelings were valuable, not for
their mere poignancy, but by their effect on the
central spirit; and he labored incessantly to express them with eloquence and yet with control.
It is only little men who estimate an emotion
by its intensity, and who try to express everything, the hysterical as well as the deliberate,
the trivial and mischievous as well as the
weighty and the inspiring.   They imagine that
success in art depends on the number of things
they say, that to voice a temperament is to build
a character.   But great men, though they reject
no sincere human feeling, care more to give the
right impression than to be exhaustive; and the
greatest feel instinctively that the last word of
their art must be constructive, positive, upbuilding.   Thoreau remarks that the singer can
easily move us to tears or laughter, but asks,
"Where is he who can communicate a pure
morning joy?"   It is Brahms's unique greatness among modern composers that he was able
to infuse his music, in which all personal passion
is made accessory to beauty, with this "pure

morning joy." His aim in writing is something more than to chronicle subjective feelings,
however various or intense. And that is why
we have to consider him the greatest composer
of his time, even though in particular depart-
ments he must take a place second to others.
Steadily avoiding all fragmentary, wayward, and
distortive expression, using always his consummate mastery of his medium and his synthetic
power of thought to subserve a large and universal utterance, he points the way for a healthy
and fruitful development of music in the future.

BIBLIOGRAPHICAL NOTE.—Of particular works of Brahms
that the reader might wish to study, here are some of the most
characteristic and well known. Piano pieces : The Waltzes, op.
39 ; the Clavierstücke, op. 76, particularly No. 2 ; the two
Rhapsodies, op. 79 ; and, in his later, more complex style, the
piano pieces, op. 116, 117, 118 and 119. Songs : Liebestreu,
op. 3, No. 1 ; Wiegenlied, op. 49, No. 4 ; the Sapphic Ode,
op, 94, No. 4 ; Standchen, op. 106, No. 1 ; Meine Liebe ist
grün, op. 63, No. 5 ; O Kuhler Wald, op. 72, No. 3. Chamber works : the two Violin Sonatas, op. 78 and 100, are among
his most genial works ; the Quartets, op. 25 and 26 ; the Trio,
op. 8 ; the Sextet, op. 18. Of his orchestral works none are
finer than the Second and Third Symphonies, the Violin Concerto,
op. 77, and the Variations on a Theme of Haydn, op. 56a. The
choral works, of which the Song of Destiny is the greatest, are
unhappily seldom given.

VIII
EPILOGUE: THE MEAN-ING OF MUSIC

VIII
EPILOGUE:
THE MEANING OF
MUSIC

—

IN the foregoing studies we have been considering, first, certain fundamental principles of musical effect in the light of which alone all special contributions to music, however various, can be understood, and second, the particular contributions of half a dozen of our contemporary composers, in which we have seen those principles exemplified. We have assumed, all along, that music is of undeniable interest to us, that it has something to say, that it is of sufficient human value to be worth studying. But now, before closing, it will be well to examine for a moment the grounds of that tacit assumption, to ask ourselves what, after all, is the reason of our interest in music. Why do we care for it? What does it mean? To such questions there

are doubtless many answers. Doubtless different hearers take different kinds of delight in it,
and its modes of appeal are as various as their
temperaments. Yet music has one sort of appeal which is deeper than all others, which indeed acts universally, and which depends on its
extraordinary power to tranquilize the heart, to
instil a peace quite magical and beyond explana-
tion. It soothes while it excites; and more
wonderful than its ability to stimulate our emotions is its power to reconcile and harmo-
nize them. And this it does without the aid of
any intellectual process; it offers us no argument, it formulates no solacing philosophy;
rather it abolishes thought, to set up in its stead
a novel activity that is felt as immediately, inexplicably grateful. To suggest how the combination of sounds can have upon us so profound an effect will be the object of this final
paper.

Mortal life, as we become acquainted with it
in experience, unshaped by any philosophic or
artistic activity, is complex, confused, and irrational. From our babyhood, when we put our
fingers in the pretty fire and draw them forth

cruelly burned, until the moment when a draught of air or the bursting of a blood-vessel suddenly arrests our important enterprises in mid-course, we constantly find our faculties, both animal and divine, encountering a world not kindly adjusted. On the material plane we find drought, frost, and famine, storm, accident, disease. On the plane of feeling and sentiment there are the separation of friends, the death of dear ones, loneliness, doubt, and disappointment; in the world of the spirit are sin and sorrow, the weakness and folly of ourselves and of others, meaningless mischance, and the caprice of destiny. In such a world, good fortune must often seem as insulting as bad, and happiness no better than misery. Where all is accidental, how can aught be significant? When our highest interests are defenceless against the onslaught, not of grave evil but of mere absurdity, how is it possible to live with dignity or hope?

Nevertheless, men have, by various means, fought sturdily against the capriciousness of life and the despair it engenders. All practical morality, to begin with, is one form of defence—comparatively a low form, but still of use. The moral man, facing the universe undaunted, asserts his own power to develop in it at least his personal particle of righteousness. As much strength as he has shall be spent on the side of order. If the world be unjust, he at least will love justice. If every one else be ruled by chance, he at least will be ruled by reason. If wicked men pursue evil, he will pursue good. From the earliest to the latest times literature has recorded such resolve. The letters of Stevenson no less than the journal of Marcus Aurelius relate the purpose of the brave individual to graft, to impress—yes, to inflict—human meaning upon an untamed universe. The stoic faith has always built on the practical power of the single man; a phrase of Thoreau's might serve for its motto: "In the midst of this labyrinth let us live a *thread* of life."

The intellect is more ambitious than the moral sense. Not content with the degree of unity a man can develop in the seething world by his single action, philosophy seeks to prove that the world itself, as a whole, deriving its nature as it must from mind, is orderly. Constructive idealism, beginning with the argument that a subject cannot truly know an object unless both are included in a higher mental organism, deduces from the common facts of consciousness the real existence of an all-inclusive Spirit. Furthermore, one of its ablest modern exponents, Professor Josiah Royce, has worked out the ethical implications of the doctrine in a way that concerns us here. He shows that the apparent irrationality of our world proceeds from the fragmentariness of our finite view, and that God, who sees his universe as a whole, must find it rational; so that " our chaos is his order, our farce his tragedy, our horror his spirituality." Were our span of consciousness widened until we could perceive the whole of existence in one thought, we should find the deep organic beauty that now we yearn for in vain. Philosophy, then, assures us both of the fundamental perfection of the world as a whole and of the inaccessibility of this perfection to us. Deeply satisfying because so sure and so ultimate, it tells us nothing of details, it has no direct word for the sorrows and the perplexities of our daily lives. It leaves us often longing for a warmer, nearer assurance of the rightness of things.

And so, to many, human love first reveals

the divine unity all are seeking. The lover reasons little about consciousness; he knows, directly and overpoweringly, that his one need is to serve the beloved. This commanding aim employs all his impulses and appetites, and he finds in pure disinterested service a peace that his own warring desires cannot invade. He comprehends for the first time his own true identity, he becomes integral and serene. Furthermore, as his love grows deeper, as it spends its inexhaustible wealth more widely, learning to take for object not only the human beloved, but all virtue and beauty, his spiritual life becomes daily larger and surer, it unifies an ever complexer body of thought and deed in its perfect organism. It acquires an alchemy with which it can dissolve even the stubborn externalities of fate; for fate itself cannot take away the power to serve, and in service love finds its joy. Renunciation, even, it never enters upon except to gain a higher good, and that essence in the soul which makes a sacrifice is one with that which in happier circumstances would enjoy. Love thus shares already the nature of religion, and confers the same benefits. In exacting entire self-surrender it bequeaths superiority to accident, an unassailable serenity. Indeed, religion is but love expanded and made universal.

Religion, then, man's final means of reading rationality in the countenance of an irrational world, is the culmination toward which the other three naturally tend. It is the natural goal of love, because he who loves the divine in one person must soon love it in all. It is the goal of science and philosophy, because these place the heart open-eyed upon the threshold of the radiant reality, where it cannot but worship. It is the natural outcome of morality, too ; for the moral man, seeing others eager for goodness, learns that the divine virtue is everywhere. And religion retains in itself the character of all these tributary insights. Like morality it prompts devotion of personal strength to the good cause ; like philosophy, it affords clarity and breadth of vision ; it is animated by the same pure, deep passion that is at the soul of love. It offers man a code of conduct, a cosmology, and an object of devotion. Surely, one would think he could ask for nothing more.

But, alas ! we are not perfect creatures, capable of living always on these heights. Hours of weariness and confusion overtake us, our glimpses of the shining cosmos fade away, and we are left groping in a formless world. The universe does not change, but our faculties become jaded, we cannot keep them at the necessary pitch. The moralist knows moods of discouragement, when his power is at ebb, and the forces of evil press him sorely, entering even his own heart in the forms of temptation, sloth, and despair. The scientist encounters facts which his schemes cannot embrace, and for the moment interprets his own limitation as a disorder in nature. The philosopher often finds the universe more than a match for his synthetic powers of thought. Love has its tragedies, and faith its hours of eclipse. Even Christ must cry out, "My God! my God! why hast thou forsaken me?" The world, in a word, is too big for us. Facing its vast whirl and glitter with our modest kit of senses, intellect, and spirit, we are blinded, deafened, dizzied, completely bewildered. And then, recalling with wistful regret our partial insights, we fancy them gone forever and ourselves wholly lost.

It is just at these moments, when the mind

momentarily fails in its unequal struggle with reality, that we discover the deep meaning and the supreme service of Art. For Art is the tender human servant that man has made himself for his solace. He has adjusted it to his faculties and restrained it within his scope; fashioning it from the infinite substance, he has impressed upon it finite form. It is a voice less thunderous than nature's, a lamp that does not dazzle like the great sun. It simplifies the wealth that is too luxuriant, and makes tangible a fragment of the great ethereal beauty no mortal can grasp. Thus art is visible and audible rightness; it is the love of God made manifest to the senses, a particular symbol of a universal harmony. When we are too weary to be comforted by the remote, abstract good that religion promises, art comes with its immediate, substantial, caressing beauty. Seeking to prove nothing, making no appeal to our logical intellects, requiring of us no activity, saying nothing of aught beyond itself, it is supremely restful. Finding us defeated in our search for rationality, it says, " Search no longer, puzzle no more; merely listen and look; see, here it is!" Its beauty answers our problems never directly, but by gently making them irrelevant.

Art, then, differs from morality, philosophy, love and religion, in that it presents directly to sense the variety in unity which they manifest only to the mind and spirit. Like them, it deals with life, but the unity that it attains by selection and exclusion is unlike their unity in being tangible. Made by man, it has this one supreme advantage, that it is adapted from the outset to his needs. What it cannot unify it can exclude. Though nature care nothing for the peculiarities of the eye, a landscape painter can omit a tree that upsets the balance of his composition. Actual men and women present all sorts of incongruities of figure, but the sculptor can suppress the stooping shoulders, the knobby hips, and the bandy legs. Language bristles with trivial and vulgar words, but no poet except Walt Whitman thinks it necessary to write about hatters, who cannot, according to Stevenson, " be tolerated in emotional verse." Out of the infinite number of sounds that besiege our natural ears, musicians have selected about ninety definite tones, preordained to congruity, with which to weave their marvelous fabric. That is ever the method of art; it excludes the irrelevant or the discordant, in order to secure a salient and pure integrity. By sacrificing something of the richness of experience, it gains a rationality unknown in experience. Browning's Pippa is a gentle, noble soul, bringing goodness everywhere; in real life she would be a poor mill-girl insulted by a thousand sordid and accidental details. Shelley portrays Beatrice Cenci in the transfiguring light of poetic truth; actual experience would show her tortured by a sinister and ignoble fate. No Greek youth could have matched the perfect plastic beauty of the Disk-thrower, and no Italian woman ever symbolized cruel, sphinx-like loveliness as does the Mona Lisa. Corot's nature is grayer and softer and more harmonious than ever existed on earth. And such songs as Schumann's "Ich Grolle Nicht" and Tschaïkowsky's "Nur Wer die Sehnsucht Kennt" pulsate with a passion as intense but far less torn and fragmentary than that by which they were inspired. This serene perfection, which wraps like a mantle all works of genuine art, results from harmonious organization, and is attained only by excluding the irrelevancies always present in nature. Whistler is wise as well as witty when he exclaims that " to ask the painter to copy nature as he sees it is to invite the pianist to sit on the keyboard." Were there, to be sure, a perfect adjustment between nature and our faculties, were we able to discern the unity that must exist even in the infinitely complex Whole of the world, then such a dictum would be outgrown, and selection would cease to be the procedure of art. But until we have grown to possess universal synthetic power art will have its solacing mission and its selective method as now.

Meanwhile it will have also, of course, its inevitable limitations. If it be more orderly than nature, it will be far less rich and various ; effects that nature presents in a bewildering drench of experience, a work of art will have to isolate and develop alone. A pictured landscape, however perfect, is but one phase of the reality ; in nature there is ceaseless play and change, mood succeeds mood, and the charm is more than half in the wayward flux and transformation. A portrait shows but one character ; a human face is a whole gallery of personalities. The wealth of experience excites even while it bewilders us, and when we turn to the work of art we unconsciously adopt a narrower standard. Primitive art especially impresses us as bare and denuded, because the primitive artist has neither technical skill nor synthetic power of thought to combine more than a few elements. Thus early painting and sculpture, in dealing with the human figure, carry delineation little further than to show man with head and body, two legs and two arms. Refinements of contour and proportion are left to be observed by later artists. Similarly the folk ballads in which poetry takes its origin confine themselves to elementary incidents and emotions. In general, rudimentary art is always so far behind nature as to seem to have hardly any connection with it at all.

As time goes on, however, art passes through an evolution, becoming gradually more potent in its treatment of reality. Its progress takes the form of a curious zigzag, the resultant of two alternating tendencies; what happens is something like this. For a while it develops its power of synthesis (a power dependent both upon technical skill in handling material and on organizing force of thought) until it is able to present a few simple factors of effect in clear, salient unity. This is what is called a period of classicism. Then, dissatisfied with its attainment, desiring a richer reflection of the great whirl of experience, it reaches out after novel effects; its vision is for a while more extended than clear, and, presenting many effects which it cannot yet unify, it becomes brilliant, suggestive, fragmentary, turgid, inchoate. There has been a sacrifice of the old simple clarity for a richer chaos, or, in the trite terminology, a romantic movement. Now, however, technical skill and synthetic power of thought again advance, and a new and complexer order supervenes on the temporary confusion. Unity of effect is regained, art is classic once more (but with increased wealth of meaning), and the time is ripe for another burst of romanticism. By this alternation of impulses art grows, and when either tendency is defective we have a diseased art. If there be no romantic movement, if art remains contented with its acquired scope, there is stagnation, pedantry, academicism; if there be no classical period of assimilation, we have vagueness and turgidity, qualities even more fatal, since, as we have seen, the justification of art is its power to clarify. The general formula for wholesome artistic advance might, then, run thus: "Increase in the variety of the selected elements, without loss of the ideal unity imposed upon them." And the ideal goal of art is a representation of the whole of life, stamped with complete unity.

Turning now to music, we must point out that, although it has in a general way undergone a development like that of the other arts, made up of alternating classic and romantic movements, it has had from the first certain advantages over them in the struggle for richness and clarity, advantages proceeding from its fundamental nature. For tones are unique in our mental experience as being at once more directly expressive of the emotional essence of life than any other art-material, and more susceptible of orderly structure.

That music is beyond all the other arts directly expressive of man's deeper passional life scarcely needs theoretic proof; the fact is in the experience of every one who has listened to a military band, to a homely song lovingly rendered, or to a ragged Hungarian with a violin. These things take a physical grip upon our emotions, they stir our diaphragms, galvanize our spines, and compel us to shiver, laugh or weep. Combined with such physical affections, moreover, are ideas of indescribable vividness and poignancy. Joy and grief, hope and despair, serenity, aspiration, and horror, fill our hearts as we listen to music. They come in their pure essence—not as qualities of something else. And this is what is meant by the familiar statement that the other arts are representative while music is presentative. Poetry, painting, and sculpture show us things outside ourselves, joyful or grievous things perhaps, hopeful or desperate or beautiful or ugly things, but still *things*. But music shows us nothing but the qualities, the disembodied feelings, the passional essences. Let the reader recall for a moment the effects of painting or of poetry, the way in which they present emotion. Is it not always by symbolism, by indirection? Does not the feeling merely exhale from the object instead of constituting the object as it does in music? In looking at a pastoral landscape, for instance, do we not first think of the peaceful scene represented, and only secondarily feel serenity itself? In reading " La Belle Dame sans Merci " is it not only by a process of associative thought that we come to shudder with a sense of unearthly and destructive passion? Yes, in the representative arts emotion is merely adjective; in music alone is it substantive. We see in a portrait a lovely woman; we behold in marble a noble youth; we read in poetry a desperate story; in music, on the contrary, we hear love, nobility, despair. And since this emotional life is the deepest reality we know, since our intuitions constitute in fact the very essence of that world-spirit which is but projected and symbolized in sky, sun, ocean, stars, and earth, music cannot but be a richer record of our ultimate life than those arts which deal with objects and symbols alone. It is the penetration, the ultimacy, of music that gives it such extraordinary power. The other arts excel it in definiteness, in concreteness, in the ability to delineate a scene or tell a story; but music surpasses them all in power to present the naked and basic facts of existence, the essential, informing passions.

A secondary and subordinate advantage of music proceeds from the nature of its material. Tones, produced and controlled by man, are far more easily stamped with the unity he desires than the objects of external nature. These are stubborn outer facts, created without regard to the æsthetic sense, and in a thousand ways un-amenable to it. The great dazzle of sunlight is too keen for human eyes, which perceive better on dim, gray days; many of nature's contours are larger than we can grasp. Every painter will tell you that there are inharmonious colors in the sunset, and one daring critic has gone so far as to impugn the " vulgarity of outline " of the American hills. It matters not whether the maladjustment indicate a fault in nature or a limitation in man; the point to note is that the representative arts deal with a material less pli-able than tones. Words, the material of poetry, occupy in this respect a curious intermediate position. Like tones, they are man-made, but, like outer objects, they are "given," fixed and indocile to man's æsthetic needs. (We remem-ber the example of the " hatter.") Though made by man, in fact, they are made not by his æsthetic but by his practical energy. They were devised, not for beautiful adjustment, but to convey thoughts, and when the poet comes and uses them to make an art he finds them almost as perverse as the painter's trees and hills. Tones, however, have no practical utility whatever; not only do they not exist outside of music, but they would be of no use if they did. Hence they may be chosen and grouped by the free æsthetic sense alone, acting without let or hindrance, except what is imposed by the thing to be expressed. For hundreds of years man has been testing and comparing, accepting and rejecting, the elements of the tonal series, with the result that we have to-day the ladder or scale of ninety-odd definitely fixed tones, out of which all music is composed. And though the series has been developed wholly by instinct, and it is only within the last half-century that the natural laws underlying it have been discovered, yet it has been built up so slowly and tentatively, and with so sure and delicate a sense of its internal structure, that it is an unsurpassable basis for complex and yet perfectly harmonious tone-combinations. In a word, the material of music is by origin self-congruous, fitted to clear structure, preordained to an order at once rich and transparent.

Preordained to beauty, then, is the musician's material: and yet the musician is not exempted from the difficulties of his brother artists. If they work in a less plastic material, he has to govern subtler and more wayward forces. He can attain a wonderful perfection, but only through unremitting labor. His task is to embody the turbulent, irrational human feelings in serene and beautiful forms. He is to master the dominating, to reconcile the warring, to impose unity on the diverse and the repellant. Mozart and Haydn might handle their art with ready ease, because their emotions were naïve; but Beethoven, who essayed to look into the stormy and tortured heart of man, found himself involved in a travail Titanic and interminable. Nevertheless he did succeed in harnessing the vast forces with which he deals, and his success is as conclusive a vindication as we could desire of music's power to deal with its profound verities. When we think of Beethoven's immortal works, immortal both by their strength and by their beauty, can we doubt that music expresses our deepest emotional nature with unrivalled fullness, and yet so reconciles it with itself as to symbolize our highest spiritual peace?

From the swelter and jungle of experience

in which it is our lot to pass our mortal days, days which philosophy cannot make wholly rational, nor love wholly capable of service, nor religion wholly serene, we are thus privileged to emerge, from time to time, into fairer realms. Tantalized with an unattainable vision of order, we turn to art, and especially to music, for assurance that our hope is not wholly chimerical.   Then

> "Music pours on mortals
> Its beautiful disdain."

Disdainful it is, truly, because it reminds us of the discord and the rhythmless onmarch of our days. It voices the passions that have torn and mutilated and stung and blinded us; we meditate the foolishness, the fatality, of our chaotic lives. But beautiful it is also ; and it has been wisely said that beauty offers us " a pledge of the possible conformity of the soul with nature." Music, at once disdainful and beautiful, shows us our deepest feelings, so wayward and tragic in experience, merged into ineffable perfection.

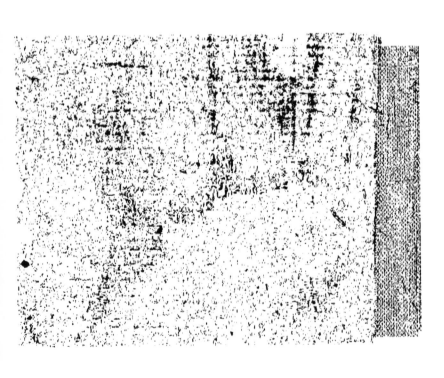